LIEUTENANT-GENERAL
SIR RALPH ABERCROMBY, K.B.

LIEUTENANT-GENERAL

SIR RALPH ABERCROMBY K.B.

1793-1801

A MEMOIR BY HIS SON

JAMES LORD DUNFERMLINE

"He was illustrious for his virtues, which were unsullied by any vice. He ruled his conduct by the motto of his family—'Vive ut Vivas;'—his death was glorious, and he died in the arms of victory." —GENERAL F. MAITLAND.

The Naval & Military Press Ltd

in association with

The National Army Museum, London

Published jointly by

The Naval & Military Press Ltd
Unit 10 Ridgewood Industrial Park,
Uckfield, East Sussex,
TN22 5QE England

Tel: +44 (0) 1825 749494
Fax: +44 (0) 1825 765701

www.naval-military-press.com
www.military-genealogy.com
www.militarymaproom.com

and

The National Army Museum, London
www.national-army-museum.ac.uk

In reprinting in facsimile from the original, any imperfections are inevitably reproduced and the quality may fall short of modern type and cartographic standards.

PREFACE.

The following Memoir of Lieutenant-General Sir Ralph Abercromby, was written by my Father during his residence at Colinton, after he had retired from official life.

His reasons for undertaking this work, and the objects which he had in view in writing it, are so fully developed by himself in the Introductory Chapter, that all further explanations by me on these points would be superfluous.

It may be right to observe, that although my Father, throughout this Narrative, has invariably given to my Grandfather the title of "Sir Ralph," by which he was most generally known, it was only on the 15th of July 1795, that the Order of the Bath, from which he derived it, was conferred upon him in acknowledgment of his services.

It only remains for me to add, that this Memoir is now printed from the original MS. of my Father, precisely as he left it.

DUNFERMLINE.

COLINTON HOUSE, *August* 1861.

CONTENTS.

	PAGE
INTRODUCTION, ...	1

CHAPTER I.
FAMILY AND EARLY LIFE, ...	13

CHAPTER II.
CAMPAIGN IN FLANDERS, ...	39

CHAPTER III.
COMMAND IN THE WEST INDIES, ...	54

CHAPTER IV.
COMMAND IN IRELAND, ...	61

CHAPTER V.
EXPEDITION TO HOLLAND, ...	139

CHAPTER VI.
EXPEDITION AGAINST CADIZ, ...	219

CHAPTER VII.
EXPEDITION TO EGYPT, ...	240

CHAPTER VIII.
CONCLUSION, ...	303
APPENDIX, ...	309
INDEX, ...	323

INTRODUCTION.

So many lives of those officers who distinguished themselves in the Army and Navy during the protracted war with France have been written, that it has repeatedly been remarked as an omission that no authoritative account of the character and services of Sir Ralph Abercromby had ever been given to the public. The obligation to secure the performance of this duty to the memory of Sir Ralph was pressed upon me by some who had formed their opinions from personal intercourse and observation, and by others, who, judging from his public acts, had a high estimate of his character, his ability, and his services. It was especially and strongly urged by one who, from his public situation, had become familiar with the history and details of the service, and with military opinions, that the army owed more to the services of Sir Ralph than to those of any other of our generals between the Duke of Marlborough and the Duke of Wellington, and that it was due to his memory that his personal character and his public conduct should be so developed as to preserve the remembrance of the zeal, ability, and devotion which he displayed in improving the discipline, elevating the character, and maintaining the renown of the English army in the arduous struggle in which the country had been engaged.

Such an appeal could only be met in a cordial spirit, and could not be dismissed without that deliberate consideration to which it was so justly entitled. Conscious of the difficulty of the task which I have undertaken, I have gladly sheltered myself under the sanction of an authority which I highly respect.

The difficulties which presented themselves, in making an effort to comply with this appeal, were most discouraging, and they will account not only for the delay in performing a duty, but also in some degree for the imperfection of this Memoir, and for the many deficiencies that cannot fail to be remarked. The delay is no doubt much to be regretted, for the interest that had been excited by the events in which Sir Ralph had borne a prominent part, has passed away; but it was unavoidable; because justice could not have been done without revealing transactions that could not have been sooner disclosed without a violation of those rules which are prescribed by respect for the feelings of individuals, and for the public interest.

The defeats and disasters which attended the first part of the French war, contrast so strikingly with the brilliant success of the Spanish campaigns and the glory of Waterloo, that it seems to be a hopeless effort to excite an interest in the life of a military officer who did not live to see the Peace of Amiens, the attainment of which was the object of the service in which he fell.

The brief military career of Sir Ralph can have little attraction for those who regard success as the only test of merit; but it may have a deep interest for those who can appreciate the virtue of an officer advanced in life who devotes himself to the service of his country from the day that war is declared to the day of his death, who is discouraged by no disappointment or defeat, who shrinks from no climate, who surrenders at a critical moment a high and honourable position, because he would not consent to oppress the people by violating the principles of law and of the Constitution, and who closed his life in the last, the most difficult, and the most arduous service of that war in which he had throughout borne so distinguished a part,—it may enable those who wish to trace the progress of the English army from the state of disorganization into which it had fallen at the commencement of the French war, to the discipline and skill which it subsequently acquired and displayed, to appreciate the efforts which were made by Sir Ralph to infuse an improved spirit into all the departments of the service.

The active military life of Sir Ralph, with the exception of having served as a subaltern officer in Germany, under Prince Ferdinand of Brunswick, from the close of the year 1758 to the end of that war, is limited to the period between the Declaration of War by France, in the year 1793, and the year 1801, when he fell in Egypt. During his foreign service in Europe, he never held the chief command, except in 1799, when the Helder and the Dutch fleet were taken, and he was then superseded by the Duke of York, and afterwards during portions of the years 1800 and 1801, when he served in the Mediterranean. Sir Ralph twice held the chief command in the West Indies, but such colonial service, however important it may be to the interests of the country, or however it may be attended with complicated difficulties, is not so well calculated to excite general interest, or to display the resources and genius which are characteristic of a distinguished commander, as the more varied and continuous operations of a continental campaign. As Sir Ralph did not court active service in the struggle for American independence, his military career did not begin until he was advanced in life, and was necessarily limited to the first portion of the war with France. It is unfortunate that Sir Ralph kept no journal of his proceedings, and maintained no regular private correspondence, in which his views and opinions might have been preserved. His correspondence, official or private, with the Ministers of the Crown, and which has been preserved, is, in consequence of his holding subordinate situations, limited to the early portion of the expedition to Holland, to his commands in Ireland and in the Mediterranean. This apparent indifference to the means by which his conduct, if necessary, might be explained or vindicated, and his reputation preserved, seems to be inconsistent with that ardent and honourable ambition which he always cherished and anxiously desired to gratify. It did not proceed from negligence or indolence, faults from which he was entirely exempt, but from his characteristic self-reliance, and from the high standard by which alone he thought that true fame ought to be tested.

He loved real fame, but he always considered that it never could be honourably earned and deserved except by those who, having been placed in a position which enabled them to perform critical or important service, and who, relying on the consciousness of their own purity and devotion, could rest their fame on the simple and unaided narrative of the events which had occurred. From a sense of the duty which as a soldier he owed to his Sovereign and to the country, he willingly gave his zealous service to the public; but with little hope that he should ever be able to realize fame that would bear the test of his own standard. This lofty ambition, so characteristic of generous and noble aspirations, led Sir Ralph to disregard all secondary means by which his fame could be extended or preserved. He neither courted popular favour nor the rewards of his Sovereign. He did not value such distinctions unless they were spontaneously conferred, and unless he felt conscious that they had been duly and justly earned by useful and solid service rendered to his country. The sincerity with which he entertained these opinions will be illustrated and confirmed by some striking passages in his life. It may be said that this is a strained and not very practical view of the subject, because it can only apply to those who have been highly gifted, and who have had an opportunity of displaying their powers. I do not deny that there is truth in this objection, but I can truly say that such were the opinions ever entertained by Sir Ralph; and I must admit that the influence of the most pure and virtuous conduct is often less useful, beneficial, and extended, when it has not been preceded by a discreet cultivation of those secondary means by which popular fame is conciliated and acquired. How numerous are the instances in which a false estimate is made of those who obtrude all their small services on the public notice, and of those who modestly, perseveringly, and honourably pursue the path of duty, and rest their hopes of fame on the judgment of the discerning few.

It was also unfortunate for Sir Ralph, that when he began his military career, the inefficiency and disorganization of the English army were such that they were wholly unprepared for the service on which they were employed. A distinguished writer and a most excellent judge has stated, "that the English army that was disposable for foreign service at the commencement of the war with France, was deplorable. The officers were without instruction; the improvement was gradual; and its regeneration can only be dated from the war in Egypt."[1] The same writer truly adds that the English soldier is distinguished by his docility and obedience, and that resignation and discipline, united with coolness and courage, are qualities to be preferred to more brilliant but less persevering valour. It is obvious, that even with such admirable materials, no energy and no skill on the part of a commander could promptly correct or remedy the evils arising from the deficient experience and instruction of the officers. Time, perseverance, judgment, and, above all, the example of the commander, were required to train the officers to a knowledge of their various duties, to the exact observance of discipline, and to a watchful and unceasing care for the wants and health of the soldiers. That Sir Ralph laboured with untiring zeal to inspire the officers under his command with an ardent desire to learn and to perform their duties, has been acknowledged by those who observed his career, and have so highly appreciated the services which he rendered to the English army, and which has been recorded in the published opinion of the Commander-in-Chief, who held him forth as an example, not only for his heroism in the

[1] General Jomini.

field, but for the not less valuable qualities of an exact observance of discipline, and for his ever-watchful attention to the health and wants of his troops.

The success of his efforts is attested by the fact, that the regeneration of an army, which he found in so deplorable a condition, can only be dated from the war in Egypt, and that he left to his successor the organized means of reaping that harvest of glory which has been gathered in the Peninsula and on the plains of Waterloo. Sir Ralph did not achieve this success by any theoretical rules or code which he promulgated, but by the steadiness and justice with which he enforced exact discipline, by never withholding censure when it was merited, by freely bestowing praise when it had been honourably earned, and by the example which he constantly gave of the exactness and spirit in which he expected that those under his command should perform all their duties.

It is comparatively an easy task to write the life of a commander whose career has been marked by general and brilliant success. It is difficult, though perhaps not less important or useful, to do justice to a commander who, in despite of the many and great disadvantages under which his course was run, and in despite of the signal failure which attended all our continental efforts during the first portion of the French war, has left a name which is still revered by the army, and has been honoured by the cordial approval of his country, of the Parliament, and of his Sovereign.

My means are most scanty, for the only very material assistance on which I have relied, is a faithful and accurate journal, which was kept, unknown to Sir Ralph, by his son, Lieutenant-General Sir John Abercromby, who acted, during the service in the Mediterranean, as Deputy Adjutant-General under Lord Hopetoun. My consolation is, that it will be admitted that there must have been virtuous qualities in the character, and real merit in the services of Sir Ralph, which enabled him, under adverse circumstances, to win the entire confidence of the Government, the respect of his brethren in arms, and to make an enduring impression on the judgment of the public. My hope is, that with the knowledge I possess, greater perhaps than that of any person now living, of the thoughts and opinions of Sir Ralph on important subjects, and with the aid of such particulars and anecdotes as I have procured, I shall be enabled to develop his real character, and to elucidate the motives and principles which influenced the whole tenor of his life. I sincerely regret, for various reasons, that the task has devolved upon me; and I have only undertaken it, because I failed in my efforts to make a satisfactory arrangement for its execution, and because I thought that it was a duty from which I ought not to shrink. I am so well aware of my inability to impart novelty and interest to the military services in which Sir Ralph was engaged, that I have not made the attempt. They have already been recorded with abundant fulness in the history of the times. My object has been to give prominence to such occurrences and events as were illustrative of his character and of his merits as a commander, and were calculated to display the manly and generous devotion to the service of his country, which animated his conduct throughout every portion of his public and private life. I have always felt that it was an objection to my engaging in this effort that I could not be relieved from the suspicion of not being an impartial judge in such a case, but I have obeyed what would have been the wish of Sir Ralph, who would have scornfully rejected those strained efforts which are often made to give importance to a biographical narrative; and he would have insisted that his conduct and character should be judged by a simple and scrupulous exposition of the services which he had performed, and of the accordance of his conduct with the principles which he uniformly professed. The facts which I have collected and recorded, cannot fail to be interesting to the descendants of Sir Ralph; and if those into whose hands this Narrative will fall shall decide that it is fit to be given to the public, they may with confidence rely on the accuracy and truth of the statements which it contains.

CHAPTER I.

FAMILY AND EARLY LIFE.

IN several imperfect and inaccurate notices of the life of Sir Ralph which have been published, the circumstances of his family have been misrepresented, and therefore it is necessary that they should now be correctly stated.

Mr. George Abercromby of Skeith, who was a distant relation of Sir James Abercromby, Baronet, of Birkenbog in Banffshire, soon after the Restoration, purchased the estate of Tullibody in the county of Clackmannan, from a family of the name of Meldrum. Mr. George Abercromby adopted as his heir Alexander, one of the younger sons of Sir James Abercromby. On the marriage of Alexander with Miss Duff, the daughter of Mr. Duff of Braco, Mr. George Abercromby made a settlement on his adopted son, and bequeathed to him the estate of Tullibody, which is now in the family of his descendants. After Alexander came into possession of the estate of Tullibody, he represented the county of Clackmannan in the Union Parliament. He was a bitter foe to the exiled family of Stuart, and a warm supporter of the Protestant succession. In religion he was a decided Presbyterian, and, from his dread of Episcopacy, he preferred a Federal to an Incorporating Union. In the year 1754, Alexander died at the advanced age of eighty-four, and was succeeded by his eldest son George, the father of Sir Ralph. George had been called to the bar, but he never prosecuted his profession, although he was considered to have acquired such a competent knowledge of law, that he was requested by Mr. Dundas, the Professor of Civil Law in the University of Edinburgh, to supply his place during a session when he was unavoidably absent. During several sessions Mr. Abercromby gave lectures in the University on the Law of Nature and Nations, having purchased that professorship, which, in accordance with the prevailing practice of the time, was treated as a subject of sale. Mr. Abercromby was distinguished for his industry, his love of knowledge, and his vigorous and comprehensive understanding. Sir Ralph often expressed his regret that his father had never been called into active life, in which he could scarcely have failed to have become useful and eminent. Mr. Abercromby, who was born in the year 1705, died in the month of May 1800, when he was within a few weeks of completing his ninety-fifth year. It is worthy of notice that both the grandfather and father of Sir Ralph lived to become by seniority the oldest members of the Scotch bar. The mother of Sir Ralph was a daughter of Mr. Dundas of Manor, and, according to all tradition, she was not less remarkable for her vivacity, the warmth of her affections, and the solidity of her understanding, than for her beauty. She commanded and retained the steady attachment of all her sons, three of whom rose to rank and eminence in their professions.

Sir Ralph was born in the month of October 1734 at Menstry, an adjoining property which had been added, by purchase, to the estate of Tullibody, and where his parents then resided. The first part of his education was judiciously directed by the Rev. Mr. Syme, who acted as his private tutor, and he was afterwards removed to the school of Mr. Moir at Alloa. That school was then highly esteemed by the Jacobite gentry of Scotland, but his father disregarded that circumstance, as he was of opinion that the school was in all other respects correctly and skilfully conducted. If Mr. Moir attempted to infuse his own peculiar views and principles into the minds of his pupils, he was signally unsuccessful in making any impression on Sir Ralph. After passing some time at the school at Alloa, Sir Ralph was sent to Rugby, where he remained until he was eighteen years of age. During the years 1752-53 he was a student in the University of Edinburgh, where he attended the moral and natural philosophy and civil law classes. A most intelligent contemporary and relative of Sir Ralph, who lived in the same house with him while he was a student in the University of Edinburgh, has thus recorded his impression of his conduct and character at this period of his life:—" Sir Ralph on leaving Rugby was manly and sensible beyond his years, of prepossessing appearance, and with polished manners. If not a hard student while attending the University of Edinburgh, he punctually performed the tasks that were required of him, and he gave much satisfaction to the professors, who regarded him as a youth of sound rather than of brilliant parts, and who bid fair to obtain distinction in the pursuits of active life. He was much respected and beloved by his companions and coevals, who admired the soundness and comprehensiveness of his intellect, accompanied by the urbanity and sweetness of his disposition." The writer of these remarks survived Sir Ralph, and saw the fulfilment of his prediction.

In the autumn of 1754, Sir Ralph was sent to Leipsic to prosecute the study of the civil law. He went to Holland in company with Lord Elgin, who had been his school-fellow at Alloa, and who was going to a French academy. At the Hague they were presented to Sir Joseph Yorke, then the British Minister in Holland, who disclosed the vigilance with which the Government watched the education of the youth of rank or fortune in Scotland, by twitting them with having been at a Jacobite school at Alloa.

On his return from Leipsic, Sir Ralph announced to his father that he had a very strong dislike to the study of the law, and that he had an ardent desire to devote himself to the military profession. This was a severe disappointment to his father, whose penetration had enabled him to discern the promising abilities of his son, which he thought were most likely to be successfully excited and displayed in the legal profession. When he found that the opinion of Sir Ralph was firm, and had been deliberately formed, his good sense led him to see that nothing was more calculated to defeat the expectations which he had cherished than perseverance in a pursuit which was uncongenial to the taste and inclination of his son, and he therefore yielded and determined to promote with cordiality his desire to devote himself to a military life. In accordance with this change of profession, a cornetcy was, in March 1756, purchased in the Third Dragoon Guards, in which regiment Sir Ralph served, in country quarters, until it was sent to Germany in the year 1758. When Sir Ralph received his first commission he possessed the advantage of a useful and liberal education, but it had in no respects been directed with reference to the profession in which he had embarked. Whatever knowledge he subsequently acquired that could be useful to a commander, was the result of private study and of his own practical observation and experience. From the first he was remarked for a zealous performance of his duties, and his attention was especially directed to the means of combining exact discipline with a judicious and considerate attention to the wants and health of the soldiers. His reason taught him that these were most useful and important elements in the formation of an efficient army, and he cultivated them assiduously throughout his life.

In Germany, his steady attention to his duty, aided by the advantage of possessing more instruction, and a more liberal education, than most of his brother officers, recommended him to the notice of General Sir William Pitt, to whom he was otherwise unknown, who selected him to be one of his aides-de-camp. In February 1760, Sir Ralph became a lieutenant in the Third Dragoon Guards, and in 1762, a troop was purchased for him; in 1770, he became major, and, in 1773, lieutenant-colonel of the regiment; and, during all that time, he served with it in Ireland. In 1780, Sir Ralph obtained the brevet rank of colonel, and, in 1781, he became colonel of the 103d or King's Irish Infantry. The 103d regiment was disbanded in 1783, when Sir Ralph retired on half-pay.

The military life of Sir Ralph has now been traced to the close of the struggle for American independence. The question may reasonably be asked, How did it happen that Sir Ralph, who had expressed so ardent a desire to devote himself to a military life, and who, at an advanced age, was eager to embark in the war with France with all the zeal and energy of youth, had never courted or obtained active employment during the war with America? The true answer is, that Sir Ralph was a sincere and honest friend of rational liberty; he sympathized with the Americans in their struggle for independence; and he ever held the moderation, the sound judgment, and the disinterested patriotism of General Washington in the highest veneration. The subsequent events of the life of Sir Ralph leave no doubt that it must have been a severe mortification to him, that the country was engaged in a war in which he could not make an effort to gratify his ardent love of distinction without a sacrifice of his feelings and his principles; but he was fortunately able to avoid a conflict between his duty as a soldier and the principles which he had adopted as a citizen, having been, during the whole course of the American War, employed in Ireland, in the discharge of regimental or staff duties.

It may, perhaps, be urged by those who think the war with France originated in a desire on the part of the sovereigns to crush the liberties of the people, and to control their right to choose their own government, that it was, therefore, similar in principle to the war with America, and consequently, that the conduct of Sir Ralph, in serving against France, is open to the charge of inconsistency. If such a charge should be made, it might be met by the fact that France declared war against England, and by reference to what passed in a debate in the

House of Commons, when the conduct and duties of officers in such cases were canvassed. Lord Howe said that, if left to his own free choice, he would have declined to serve against the Americans. Other officers shared the opinion of Lord Howe, but acted with more decision. Admiral Keppel had said that, although professional employment was the dearest object of his life, he could not accept it in the line of America. Lord Effingham, on his regiment being ordered to America, wrote to the Secretary at War,—" I cannot, without reproach from my own conscience, consent to bear arms against my fellow-subjects in America, in what, to my discernment, is not a clear cause;" and resigned his commission. General Conway, recognising the correctness of these opinions, urged that there was a material distinction between a foreign war, where the whole community was involved, and a domestic war on points of civil contention, where the community was divided against itself. In the first case, no officer ought to call in question the justice of his country. In the latter case, before he drew his sword against his fellow-subjects, he ought to examine his conscience whether the cause was just.

Sir Ralph had no doubt as to the decision which he ought to make with respect to the American struggle; but when France declared war against England, he obeyed, as a soldier, the call of his country, and although, from the close of the first campaign, he strenuously advised that no favourable opening for negotiation should be lost, yet he steadily maintained that war, judiciously and successfully conducted, was the surest way to obtain a safe and honourable peace.

It would be an entire misconception of the character of Sir Ralph, to conclude, from his having avoided active service in the American War, that he was biassed either by political or party feelings or attachments, or by heated or exaggerated opinions. Nothing could be further from the truth than such a supposition. He wished to lead the life of a soldier, and to place his services, on all fitting occasions, at the command of his country. He rarely mingled in the society, and never participated in the warfare of politicians, and his real sentiments were scarcely known beyond the circle of his family and a few chosen friends. This reserve did not proceed from selfish caution; but, as he reflected earnestly, deeply, and wisely on the passing events of his time, he was well aware that the opinions he had formed would either not have been acceptable to, or would not have been understood in the military circle in which he lived. He had no reserve in his intercourse with his private friends, and with those who, from their knowledge or abilities, commanded his respect and confidence; and subsequently, when he was employed during the war with France, he expressed his opinions to the Ministers of the Crown with the utmost freedom, and to an extent that was not always palatable to those to whom they were addressed.

Before entering on the private life of Sir Ralph, during the interval of peace between the close of the American and the commencement of the French War, it is necessary to state that in the year 1773 he was chosen to represent the county of Clackmannan in Parliament. The contest was severe, and was conducted by Colonel Erskine, the brother of the restored Earl of Mar, with unusual violence. Colonel Erskine published a pamphlet in which he reflected on the conduct of Lord Kennet, who was one of the Judges of the Court of Session, in terms which Sir Ralph thought ought to be resented; and as Lord Kennet could not as a Judge vindicate his own character, Sir Ralph decided that under the circumstances it became him, on behalf of Lord Kennet, who was his supporter and near relation, to assume that duty. A hostile meeting ensued, shots were exchanged, when the seconds interfered; but Sir Ralph considered that the provocation given by Colonel Erskine was so unjustifiable, that he declined to be reconciled to his opponent. Sir Laurence Dundas, who was at that time desirous of acquiring political power in Scotland, decided the contest by exercising his influence in favour of Sir Ralph, under the expectation that by so doing he became entitled to control the votes in Parliament of the candidate whom he supported. There was not the very slightest foundation for this expectation on the part of Sir Laurence; and, accordingly, Sir Ralph resented his interference, and a breach between them ensued. Although Sir Ralph resisted the assumed right of control, he did not forget the obligation which he owed to Sir Laurence for his support. He repaid it, by uniformly voting for the son of Sir Laurence in his repeated and severe contests for the county of Stirling, which were so close as to make a single vote of real value, and that at a time when there was no agreement in their political opinions, and when Sir Ralph was strongly urged by personal friends to take a different part. It may seem strange to attach any importance to a single vote in a county election, but those who know what the state of the representation of Scotland was before the passing of the Reform Bill, will be competent to appreciate the value of one vote in a keenly contested county, and in a narrow locality, in which the political conduct of every individual is known and canvassed.

A parliamentary life had no attractions for Sir Ralph, who was not prepared to surrender his judgment to the guidance of a party leader, and who thought that his services as a soldier belonged exclusively to his country. He speedily resolved never to be re-elected, and he was only restrained from resigning his seat by the feeling that doing so would have been ungracious and ungenerous towards those friends who had made great efforts and sacrifices to secure his return. Sir Ralph might have been re-elected in 1788, but he declined in favour of one of his brothers. In 1797, he was actually re-elected without his concurrence, and during his absence from the country, but immediately on his return he vacated in favour of his brother, General Sir Robert Abercromby.

A knowledge of the private habits and pursuits of any individual who has become eminent by his abilities or services, is a natural and reasonable object of desire. Details of private life ought, however, to be selected with discretion, and so limited as to be sufficient to convey a general and just impression of the character of the individual, and of his resources when in retirement. The mother of Sir Ralph died in the year 1767, and in the autumn of that year he married Miss Menzies, second daughter of Mr. Menzies of Fernton, in the county of Perth. After his marriage the whole scheme of his private life was regulated by devotion to the comfort of his father, who resided constantly in the family of his son until his death in the year 1800. "I have often reflected," says an accurate observer, "on the unmeasured and never-failing devotion of Sir Ralph and Lady Abercromby to the comfort and happiness of a parent whose life was so unusually prolonged, as an admirable and beautiful trait in their character. Such conduct is the more worthy of commendation when it is recollected that devotion to the comfort of an aged parent not only regulated but necessarily imposed many restraints on their own inclinations and course of life." According to this arrangement, Sir Ralph's residence with his family during the continuance of the American War was limited to such periods of time when he could be spared from his military duties in Ireland. The only occasion on which Lady Abercromby accompanied Sir Ralph to Ireland was during the short time he held the chief command in that country in 1798. When peace with America was concluded, and Sir Ralph had no longer any military duties to perform, he retired into a life of strict privacy, and during the interval between the close of the American War and the commencement of the war with France, he passed his time at first entirely in the country, and subsequently it was divided between the country and Edinburgh.

In the country his habits were retired and simple; he found active occupation in the management of a small farm; he acquired an interest in the different schemes of agricultural improvement which then engaged the attention of the public; he read the remarkable publications of the day, and he possessed an inexhaustible resource in his own reflections, as he was at all times rather a profound thinker than an extensive reader. His society was limited to a small circle of relations and friends, and to the neighbouring gentry and clergy, with whom he at all times associated on courteous and friendly terms. In his intercourse with his neighbours he always endeavoured to lead the conversation so as to induce his guests to express their opinions on those subjects on which they were likely to be best informed, and this they were the more readily induced to do from the singular affability and modesty of his own manner. His guests retired not only pleased with the hospitality and kindness with which they had been received, but the skill with which he had elicited whatever information each could contribute, had placed them on such good terms with themselves, that few reflected or were conscious that they had been engaged in conversation with one who was so much their superior in the extent of his views and the vigour of his understanding.

The impression made by the conduct of Sir Ralph in his retirement attracted the notice of a traveller in Scotland, to whom he was unknown. "As a country gentleman," says the writer, "Sir Ralph was ever attentive to all within the circle of his movement; he stands high in the estimation of his neighbours and dependants, and when his military glory shall have fallen into oblivion, it will be gratefully remembered that he was the friend of the destitute poor, the patron of useful knowledge, and the promoter of education among the meanest of his cottagers; and as a circumstance it may be mentioned that, in the village of Tullibody, on his paternal estate, a reading school, under his inspection, was established many years back."

Gratitude and affection may, perhaps, justify an

allusion to another of Sir Ralph's pursuits during his retirement in the country. For a considerable period of time he regularly devoted a portion of each day to the instruction of his son, the writer of this Memoir. Sir Ralph had not kept up the knowledge of Greek which he had acquired at school, but Cicero, Horace, Cæsar, Tacitus, and Livy, were authors with whom he was familiar, whose merits he tasted, and always read with real pleasure. His efforts as a teacher were mainly directed to the perusal and study of these Latin authors whom he so much admired, and to the formation of a simple, clear, and nervous style in English composition. The most vivid and enduring impression that survives, is the remembrance of the wise, elevated, and noble principles which he uniformly and earnestly inculcated, and now, at the close of a long life, a comparison of the lessons which he taught, with the results of personal experience, derived from intercourse with public men and the world, renders it impossible not to be filled with increased veneration for the penetration, sagacity, rectitude, and generous principles of the instructor, and with a painful consciousness of the manifold deficiencies of the pupil.

When Sir Ralph went to Edinburgh, his principal

object was the education of his family. He lived in a small and select society, and found occupation for his mind in the study of such subjects as interested him. During one winter he attended the Lectures on Church History, which were delivered by Dr. Hardy, who, at that time, enjoyed great reputation as one of the Professors in the University.

In his retirement Sir Ralph relied mainly on his own resolution and resources. He allowed no indulgence, and no habits of indolence to impair the energy and activity of his mind; he cherished and retained in all the freshness of youth, the ambition, and devotion to the service of his country, which had been so long kept in abeyance, but were so promptly displayed when they could, consistently with his principles, be called into action.

The French Revolution was an event which subjected the political principles, the sagacity, and the grasp of mind, of all who were capable of reflecting and reasoning on such a striking occurrence, to a severe and searching test. Some hailed it with unhesitating joy, as the assured triumph of principles which were to place the freedom and happiness of the French people on the firmest basis. Others, being attached to ancient institutions, were dismayed by the fierce inroad of Democracy, which they regarded as subversive of law, order, religion, and regulated freedom, and they became its uncompromising foes. There was a third party, who, cordially sympathizing with the French people in their desire to emancipate themselves from the abuses and vices of the old government of France, regarded this sudden and violent change with trembling anxiety, from the fear that those who had so long groaned under the iron hand of despotism, must be ill qualified to reconstruct their government with prudence and wisdom. As Sir Ralph, according to an admission of Lord Camden (which will be afterwards cited), was a person who thought "deeply and wisely" on all subjects that came under his observation, it is desirable to show what were the feelings, hopes, and fears with which he regarded the first movement of this great and startling event. Sir Ralph had anxiously watched the progress, and carefully studied the causes and results of the American revolution; he admired the conduct and character of General Washington as a noble example of moderation and patriotism, and he rejoiced in the development of the great principles of religious and civil freedom, which he always expected would exercise a powerful and favourable influence in Europe.

With such opinions, he could not fail to be warmly interested and strongly excited by the striking events of the French Revolution. From the first he made a just estimate of the importance and magnitude of the crisis that had arisen. His ardent love of liberty was tempered by a calm and sound judgment; he never was seduced by theories, however plausible; his views were practical, and he knew that freedom could not be suddenly and safely conceded to people who had been long oppressed, and that they could only be trained to the use and enjoyment of it by experience, and under the influence and control of energetic and wise leaders. He never was for a moment dazzled or misled by the professions of the leaders of the French Revolution, whose conduct he condemned as rash and dangerous in conceding to the people liberties which they were unprepared to understand or to use with discretion. His hopes for the establishment of freedom in France were always damped by the fear that liberty would be abused, and that from aiming at too much they would fail in obtaining those real benefits which were practical, and adapted to the circumstances of their situation, and which might be secured under firmer and wiser guidance. When the French Revolution was discussed in his presence, he gave expression to these sentiments, by remarking, that the French people were not sufficiently instructed to submit to the sober guidance of a Washington, and that they required to be controlled by a firm and energetic hand, such as that of Frederick of Prussia, until they could be gradually trained to the exercise of freedom; since, if they were not so restrained, the result might be perilous to themselves, might obstruct the progress of freedom, and involve the rest of Europe in serious embarrassments.

The early impressions of Sir Ralph with respect to the French Revolution are material, as they may be compared with, and may illustrate the opinions which he subsequently expressed during the progress of the War, when he was unremittingly engaged in the service of his country. The popular feeling which had been evoked throughout the country, by the writings of Paine, by the captivating professions of popular leaders, and the efforts of the indiscreet friends and admirers of the French Revolution, afforded to Sir Ralph, before he went on active service, an opportunity of expressing his opinion as to the spirit in which it ought to be met by a just and wise government. He held it to be an established truth that opinions, however delusive or erroneous, could not be controlled or put down by legislative or physical force, but that they might be successfully met and counteracted by diffusing instruction and wholesome principles among the people, in a form likely to be effective, if skilfully regulated by the standard of their knowledge and understanding. So long as he believed that the arm of force would not be extended in any direction, in the vain attempt to crush opinions, he confidently cherished the hope that good would follow from the political discussions that had arisen. He believed that a more familiar and instructed acquaintance with the merits of our institutions, and with the principles on which they were founded, would give them a stronger hold on the attachment of the people, that many of those who had been seduced by popular fallacies would be restrained, and that if some were still incorrigible, and might be led to commit acts of violence, they would easily be repressed by the ordinary laws, and with the general approbation of all classes.

With this view, he departed from his uniform practice of abstaining from all participation in political affairs, and became an active member of an association that was formed in Edinburgh for the purpose of diffusing useful information among the people. He was so satisfied with the benefits that resulted from this measure, that when he was Commander-in-Chief in Ireland in 1798, he earnestly, but in vain, recommended that a similar plan should be adopted by the Irish Government. This calm and temperate view of the crisis mortified and offended those, who, under the influence of unreasonable alarm, were urging on a mischievous policy, founded on intolerance and violence, which has left painful recollections, and fixed an indelible stain on the social and judicial history of Scotland. Sir Ralph was well aware that his opinions, however guardedly expressed, were exaggerated and misrepresented by the heated and exclusive alarmists, but he was convinced of the soundness of his views, and pursued his course with unshaken constancy. He carefully abstained from whatever was calculated to justify offence, but he never failed to mark, on fit occasions, his decided disapprobation of the intolerant and exclusive policy which was so generally recommended and adopted. An instance or two, though trifling in themselves, will illustrate the character of the times, and the temper and spirit which animated the conduct of Sir Ralph.

An able and distinguished Scotch nobleman, who had taken a warm and prominent part in defence of the French Revolution, happened to come to Edinburgh, where he was deserted and avoided by most of his former acquaintances and friends. Sir Ralph, thinking that such intolerance was calculated to be very mischievous in its consequences, and that exclusion from society was not justified by differences of opinion on political subjects, marked his disapproval of this conduct by doing an act of courtesy to a nobleman with whom he had no previous acquaintance, and the object of which could not be mistaken under the circumstances in which it was tendered. The compliment was strongly felt, and always kindly remembered, by the individual to whom it was paid.

Among those who had espoused the cause of popular reform was a young nobleman, Basil Lord Daer, who was distinguished, not only from his rank and fortune, but by the abilities and the integrity of his character, which was above all reproach, and who left a name which was long revered by the people of Scotland, who justly appreciated his sympathy with their feelings and interests, and his sincere desire to promote their comfort and to raise and improve their condition. Sir Ralph, believing that Lord Daer acted under the influence of pure and honourable principles, was anxious to ascertain the extent and the character of the views and opinions which he had adopted.

An arrangement was made by which they met at dinner at the house of a distant relative of Sir Ralph. The only persons present were Lord Daer, Sir Ralph, our host, and myself, then in my sixteenth year. The conversation was protracted, was conducted with calmness, and with that mutual respect which resulted from the conviction that both were uninfluenced by personal objects, and were actuated only by benevolent and patriotic motives. Lord Daer made a very favourable impression as to the sincerity and purity of his character, and Sir Ralph readily overlooked the exaggeration of some of his views and opinions, which he attributed to the ardour and generosity of youth, and which would be corrected by experience. Sir Ralph was always pleased when he heard young men expressing sentiments favourable to freedom, and he used to say that unless the opinions of a young man of twenty had a tinge of republicanism, he would be sure to be a corrupt man at forty. Lord Daer did not long survive, having died at an early age.

Sir Ralph was soon called away from these calm and contemplative pursuits to engage in a succession of military employments, to which, with brief intervals of repose, the remainder of his life was devoted.

CHAPTER II.

CAMPAIGN IN FLANDERS.

1793 TO 1794.

THE National Convention of France declared war against England and Holland on the 1st of February 1793. Whatever differences of opinion may have existed among statesmen or the public as to the policy or justice of the attack on France by the continental sovereigns, or as to the sincerity and skill with which the English Ministers had endeavoured to avert the calamity of war, there was no doubt that after the French declaration, it was the duty of every loyal subject to support the interest and honour of his country. Sir Ralph accordingly felt that the time had at length arrived when he could heartily embark in the active duties of his profession. Although then about to enter the sixtieth year of his age, he did not hesitate to recommence his active professional life, which had been so long suspended. He embraced the opportunity with ardour, and was animated by the hope that he might still achieve distinction by his military skill, and by his zealous devotion to the service of his country.

At this time Sir Ralph had seen no service in the field, except during his early years, when he was a subaltern officer, and afterwards when he acted as aide-de-camp to Sir W. Pitt, who held a command in the English force that was sent to Germany, and was placed under the command of Prince Ferdinand of Brunswick. The events of the War of 1756 could not fail to arrest the attention of every military student, and the frequency with which Sir Ralph recurred in conversation to the character and conduct of Frederick of Prussia, showed how closely he had observed the career of that distinguished sovereign. Prince Ferdinand of Brunswick was an able and esteemed commander, and has been especially commended for his minute and watchful attention to the comforts and health of his soldiers, an example which was rigidly followed by Sir Ralph. The rank which Sir Ralph held at the commencement of the War of 1793, was that of major-general, and the only command to which he could aspire was that of a brigadier, in the event of an English force being sent to serve on the Continent. However highly the abilities of Sir Ralph may have been respected and esteemed by those with whom he had lived in habits of intimacy, and with whom he had been associated on home service, yet from the circumstance of his having taken no part in the American War, and from his having latterly passed so many years in privacy, he was unknown to the public, and he had still to lay the foundation of his fame as a commander in the field. The Ministers having determined to send an auxiliary force to co-operate with the Allies in the Low Countries, the command of the British troops was confided to the Duke of York, and Sir Ralph was appointed to the command of a brigade to be employed in the same service.

It is not now proposed to investigate the causes which dashed the hopes that were inspired by these events, or to criticise the conduct of commanders and cabinets. All that is necessary for the present object is a brief reference to those occasions on which the British Army was brought into action during this campaign, and in which Sir Ralph bore a part. The opportunities for exertion which were offered to Sir Ralph were few, and the last, which was the most important, and the best calculated to display his energy, and his fortitude, under circumstances the most mortifying and painful, was his conduct during the retreat from Holland in the winter of 1794-95. On the 25th of February 1793, the Duke of York embarked, with three battalions of the Guards, for Holland, with the intention to relieve Williamstadt, which was then besieged by the French. The brigade to the command of which Sir Ralph was appointed, was composed of the 14th, 37th, and 53d regiments, and with them he embarked at Leith on the 21st of March; and thus it happened that the 21st of March was the day on which he entered on a new course of military service, and was also the day on which it was closed by the mortal wound which he received in the Battle of Alexandria in 1801.

The first account of the state of his brigade is to be found in the letters of Sir Henry Calvert, aide-de-camp to the Duke of York, which have been published. Writing on the 9th of April 1793, he says, that the Guards anchored off Antwerp, and that a brigade, consisting of the 14th, 37th, and 53d, under Major-General Abercromby, disembarked from their transports at the ferry opposite Antwerp, and he adds, "On the junction of the Brigade of the Line, we remarked with concern that the recruits they had lately raised were, in general, totally unfit for service, and inadequate to the fatigues of a campaign, being mostly either old men or quite boys, extremely weak and short." In a letter dated on the 26th April, Sir H. Calvert again refers to the brigade in these terms :—" I am sorry to say that our small force is much diminished by two of the regiments in the Second Brigade being totally unfit for service, so much so, that the Duke of York has left the 37th and 53d at Bruges and Ostend. The recruits that were sent to complete them immediately before their embarkation are worse than any I ever saw, even at the close of the American War, and I sincerely hope the representation of the Duke of York may awaken the resentment of the King against whatever person or persons the fault lies with. In the meantime, it is a most cruel circumstance for the officers who command these regiments, and for Major-General Abercromby, whose brigade is for the present placed quite *hors de combat.*" In a subsequent letter, Sir Henry says, "The recruits for Major-General Abercromby's brigade arrived a few days ago ; they much resemble Falstaff's men, and were as lightly clad as any Carmagnol battalion." This description of the brigade, to the command of which Sir Ralph was appointed, amply supports the statement of General Jomini, who says that the state of the English Army at the commencement of the War was deplorable, and that its regeneration was only to be dated from the War in Egypt.

It would be irksome and unprofitable to trace the progress of the English army from the landing in Holland in 1793, to the period of their final retreat from the Continent in the early part of 1795. During the whole of these campaigns Sir Ralph zealously discharged his duty, and gradually and steadily acquired the respect and confidence of his commander, and of the Army. His conduct was peculiarly distinguished in the attack on the Camp of Furnes, in the month of May 1793. In the *Gazette,* in which an account of the action is given, it is stated:—"The troops of the different nations displayed the utmost firmness and intrepidity in this arduous undertaking. The British troops who had the opportunity of distinguishing themselves were the Brigade of the Line, namely, the 14th and 53d regiments, with the Battalion formed from three light infantry and grenadier companies, commanded by Major-General Abercromby." Sir Ralph commanded the British troops who were employed in storming Valenciennes; after the surrender of which place, the Allies, instead of following up this advantage, and pressing on the French army, which was composed of raw and undisciplined recruits, determined to divide their forces, and to pursue their own separate objects.

The Duke of York received instructions from England, directing him to undertake the siege of Dunkirk. With whom this unhappy project originated, seems never to have been ascertained, and it was never either encouraged or approved by the Duke of York, or those in whom he confided. The author of the *Victoires et Conquêtes* does not hesitate to say, that France owed its safety, at that critical moment, to the decision which led to the separation of the Allied forces. The plan of the English Cabinet was bad, and the means that ought to have been provided by the Minister for its execution were criminally defective. "That this undertaking," says Sir H. Calvert, "received no countenance nor moral co-operation appeared very extraordinary. This remissness on the part of Government excited much indignation in the Army, and no small astonishment among our Allies." In France, the defeat of the attack on Dunkirk diffused universal joy, restored confidence, and aroused throughout the nation a determined spirit of resistance to the interference and dictation of foreigners, which was honourable to the French people and formidable to their enemies.

In the varied, and not very important events that occurred during the remainder of the campaign, the conduct of the Duke of York and of the British Army was irreproachable and creditable.

It was at the close of this campaign that Sir Ralph, in writing to Mr. Secretary Dundas, stated it to be his opinion, that a spirit was abroad which would certainly spread, and which could not be put down by force, and that it would be sound wisdom on our part to seize the earliest opportunity of withdrawing from the War. His opinion was, that the old monarchies were worn out, and that a new order of things was approaching, which would be felt throughout Europe. This, like many other predictions, was sound, but it was announced too soon. After the lapse of sixty eventful years, the struggle which Sir Ralph anticipated is still in progress and undecided.

The sovereigns triumphed in the War; they made a settlement of Europe which is crumbling; they violated their pledges to the people; and they only sustain themselves by mutual co-operation, by restraining the liberty of the press, by a detestable police, and large armies. In spite of all this force, opinion is making its way; some countries have gained solid advantages, others are struggling for freedom, and the ultimate result cannot be doubtful.

At the opening of the campaign, the Emperor of Germany took the command in person, and reviewed the Allied army, then in West Flanders, on the heights above Cateau. On the morning of the 17th April, the Allied army advanced in eight columns. The fourth and fifth columns were placed under the command of the Duke of York : the former he kept under his own direction, and the latter he confided to Sir William Erskine. The object of the Duke was to attack with the column under his immediate command the redoubts and village of Vaux and also the Bois de Bohain, which the enemy had strongly entrenched.

After the necessary arrangements had been made, the attack was commenced by the advanced guard under the command of Sir Ralph, in which, although the enemy's fire was very severe, he completely succeeded. The whole of a very complicated movement having proved successful, the Duke of York expressed his approbation to the army for its conduct in a general order, in which he thanks Sir Ralph "for the zeal, activity, and spirit with which he led the advanced guard of his column ;" and, in his despatch, which was published in the

Gazette, His Royal Highness repeats his obligations to Sir Ralph for his conduct on that day. On the 14th of May, the French made an attack, which they supported with desperate valour, on General Kaunitz, but they were repulsed with a most severe loss both of officers and men, and were obliged to recross the Sambre. Encouraged by this success, the Austrians determined to make an effort to expel the French from those parts of the Austrian territories of which they had taken possession. When the Austrians had formed their plan, it was unfortunately betrayed to the enemy, and the failure which ensued was by them attributed to that circumstance, though it appears that there were other causes sufficient to account for the unsuccessful result of the attack.

The Austrians approached towards the enemy on the night of the 16th of May, with the intention of attacking them at daybreak. The army was divided into five columns. Two of these divisions were directed to force a passage across the river Marque, which, indeed, they effected, but in so tired and exhausted a state that they were unable to execute the remaining portion of their orders. A third division advanced as ordered, but found the enemy in such force that they retired to their former position. The two divisions under General Otto and the Duke of York were more successful, and drove the French from several of their posts. In the last of these which was taken by the Duke's division, the enemy were strongly entrenched and made a formidable resistance, " but by the judicious conduct of General Abercromby, and the valour of the troops under his command, the entrenchment was forced and the enemy totally routed." On the morning of the 18th, the French made an attack on the column of the Duke of York, which had been weakened by a detachment sent to make a diversion in favour of those who were most severely pressed by the enemy. The French were greatly superior in numbers, and the Duke of York found himself so surrounded that he was unable to join those portions of his own troops, which were under the command of Sir Ralph and General Fox; it was with great difficulty that he escaped falling into the hands of the enemy, and succeeded in making his way to General Otto.

Sir Ralph and General Fox effected the retreat of their respective corps in a manner which is uniformly mentioned with the greatest praise in every account that has been published of the proceedings of that day. One account says:—" It was with prodigious efforts that Generals Abercromby and Fox found means to restore sufficient order among the troops to save them from utter destruction and effect a retreat. But even this was attended with almost insurmountable difficulty, the enemy pressing upon them with incessant fury, and giving them no time to recover from their forlorn situation, into which they had been thrown by the unexpected immensity of the numbers with which they had to contend on this unfortunate day." Another account mentions that the Duke of York directed General Abercromby to retire from Mouveau to the heights behind Robaix, where it was his intention to have assembled his troops. In consequence of these directions General Abercromby began his retreat, but on his arrival on the heights of Robaix, he found himself surrounded on all sides, so that the re-assembling of the Army on that position was impossible; he therefore continued his march to Lannoy, which he effected amidst the repeated attacks of the enemy who poured upon him from all quarters, and at every avenue or pass had guns ready to flank him and cavalry to attack him whenever the ground would admit. On his arrival at Lannoy he found it also in possession of the enemy, and was obliged to avoid the town, and march round it under a very heavy fire, and with much difficulty reached Templeuve.

As the object of this brief Memoir is strictly confined to the detail of such incidents as tend to illustrate the personal character and conduct of Sir Ralph, it would be superfluous to enlarge on the events of the disastrous campaign of 1794. It is only necessary to say that so long as the Army was under the command of His Royal Highness the Duke of York, there never was the slightest ground for imputing any of those disasters to the want of energetic co-operation, or to any deficiency in military conduct on the part of the Duke of York and of the British Army. On every occasion the English soldiers maintained their character for ardour, perseverance, and indomitable courage, and only retired when they were overcome by the overwhelming amount of the French force. The defeats of the Austrians, who were compelled to re-cross the Rhine, and the fall of all the fortresses in rapid succession, compelled the Duke of York to abandon Flanders, and to retire into Holland.

The defence of Holland became impracticable from the severity of the season; and that of Walcheren, which was intrusted to Sir Ralph, was rendered equally hopeless by the early setting in of a winter of most unusual severity, which enabled rivers to be easily crossed on the ice. Deprived by this circumstance of the expected means of defending themselves, nothing remained for our army but to evacuate Holland. On the return of the Duke of York to England, the chief command of the British force was placed in the hands of General Harcourt, who appears to have been unequal to such a crisis. The privations and sufferings of the Army were dreadfully aggravated by the unusual and extreme inclemency of the weather, and by the constant pressure of a victorious and superior enemy.

Under these circumstances, the duty of protecting the Army during its retreat through Holland devolved on Sir Ralph, and he was so commonly regarded as the chief commander, that some of his friends in England, not foreseeing that in the midst of these disasters, he was earning an European reputation, remonstrated with the Government for allowing him to be considered as exercising a responsibility which in fact belonged to another. The hideous details of this disastrous retreat have been so often given to the public, that it would be painful and superfluous to repeat them, and the more so as nothing new can be added.

The judgment with which the retreat was effected,

attracted general attention, and commanded respect for the constancy and ability which were displayed by those who conducted it. Infinitely the largest share of this public approbation was by common consent assigned to Sir Ralph, and his character as a commander was established.

CHAPTER III.

COMMAND IN THE WEST INDIES.

1795 TO 1797.

THE Government in England having decided to attack the French and Dutch possessions in the West Indies, a large armament, amounting at least to 15,000 men, was prepared in the autumn of 1795 for that service, and was placed under the command of Sir Ralph Abercromby. The fleet was under the orders of Admiral Christian. The convoy sailed on the 28th of November. This expedition was destined to encounter a storm of unusual length and severity. The fleet was entirely dispersed, some ships making their way to the West Indies, and the remainder scattered in all directions.

The "Glory," in which Sir Ralph sailed with Admiral Christian, kept at sea as long as possible, but was ultimately obliged, after a vain struggle of seven weeks, and after having been exposed to the very greatest danger, to return to port. This was of course most disappointing and disheartening to

Sir Ralph, but Admiral Christian in writing to a friend remarks, " that his demeanour on this occasion was so calm and composed, that it was an example to be admired and followed by all who witnessed it." The following anecdote is of no importance, but as it has been preserved by others as characteristic, I have inserted it. At a moment when the " Glory" was known to be in the most imminent danger, the confidential servant of Sir Ralph rushed into the cabin where he was with Admiral Christian, and addressing him said, " We are going to be drowned." " Very well," replied Sir Ralph, " you go to bed."

After the return of the "Glory" to port, Sir Ralph again sailed for his destination in the " Arethusa" frigate, commanded by Captain Wooley. On his arrival in the West Indies, Sir Ralph commenced the campaign by an attack on St. Lucie, in which he succeeded. He sent a force to take Demerara and Berbice, which the Dutch not unwillingly surrendered, and he also took the necessary measures for relieving St. Vincent's, and laying the foundation for the restoration of order in that Island and in Grenada.

Thus ended the first campaign in the West Indies, all having been accomplished that was possible after the serious difficulties and disasters which the fleet had encountered at its commencement.

On the conclusion of this first campaign, Sir Ralph returned to Europe in the "Arethusa," in which frigate he again sailed for the West Indies at the end of the year 1796. War with Spain having in the interval been declared, Sir Ralph was directed to attack the Spanish possessions of Trinidad and Porto Rico. The attack on Trinidad, which eventually proved successful, appears to have been considered by the King's Ministers especially desirable, because it was a place of refuge for democratic agitators, chiefly French, who instigated disturbances in our West Indian possessions. Sir Ralph was instructed, if he should find that he could not afford to leave a sufficient force for the protection of Trinidad without endangering the security of our islands, to destroy as far as possible everything that could be useful. He himself certainly took a wider view of the real importance of Trinidad, as affording facilities for any enterprise in which we might engage for the liberation of Spanish America.

In a letter from Trinidad, dated 28th February 1797, he says, "In my official letter I had the honour of giving you the detail of our operations against this island. Every part of the conduct of the Spanish troops, both by sea and land, seems to indicate a decayed nation, and to point out the possibility of further conquests, if we were in a condition to keep what we might acquire, with a small additional force. It appears necessary to keep possession of Trinidad as an important post should the war continue, for which purpose I shall leave a garrison that will be sufficient for its defence. The inhabitants are a mixture of Spanish, English, and French. I shall endeavour as much as possible to gain them by a mild and equal government."

The independence of South America was at all times a favourite project of Sir Ralph, and the further conquests to which he alludes as to be made from Trinidad, have, no doubt, reference to the continent of America, and the means by which he proposed to retain them with an inconsiderable force, were a declaration of independence, and the establishment of "a mild and equal government."[1]

After the surrender of Trinidad, which he placed under the care of Colonel, afterwards Sir Thomas Picton, whom he selected as the person best qualified to understand and appreciate his future views,

[1] *Vide* Appendix for Minute on this subject.

he proceeded to Porto Rico, the possession of which had been considered by the King's Ministers to be important, as it might afford the means of providing for those persons in St. Domingo who were living under the protection of the English Government. It seems to have been a project, which would have been difficult of execution, even if the place had been taken. The attack on Porto Rico, however, was unsuccessful. Sir Ralph, in a private letter, explains very simply and clearly the cause of his failure. He says, "Perhaps the expedition has been undertaken too lightly. We had not sufficient information, and to say the truth, it is not easily obtained. Mariners, smugglers, and merchants, generally know little but their own affairs; it is only from military men, or men of great observation, that proper information can be got. Abbé Raynal passes for a writer of little credit, but in this instance he has been correct. At all events, after the reduction of Trinidad, the Admiral agreed with me, that something further was to be done, and as both he and I had received re-inforcements, and had been instructed to attempt Porto Rico, we determined to try our fortune, trusting a little to the weakness of the enemy. We found them well prepared, with a garrison more numerous than us, and with a powerful artillery. The troops, indeed, were of the worst composition, but behind walls, they could not fail to do their duty."

The conduct of Sir Ralph at Porto Rico was most cordially approved by the Ministers, and there is no indication that his failure ever gave him any uneasiness; he considered the case to be so clear, that there was no room for difference of opinion.

Sir Ralph very much disliked the command in the West Indies, as it involved a responsibility, especially as to public expenditure, which was very irksome to him, and on the 28th of February 1797, he wrote as follows to Mr. Secretary Dundas :—

"With every wish to do my duty to the public, and to show my gratitude for the favours I have received, I hope that it will not be considered as a deviation from that principle, to ask permission to return to Europe after the campaign. I do not complain of want of health, but I find the complex nature of the civil and military duties of a commander too much for me, and I cannot discharge both completely to my satisfaction. The control of the Army accounts, and the disagreeable task of keeping within due bounds the different departments, occupy much of my time, and give me much uneasiness. When I have a little leisure I hope to simplify this business, and make matters less a load on my successor."

Sir Ralph's request was complied with, and General Cuyler was sent out to succeed him, and he returned to England.

CHAPTER IV.

COMMAND IN IRELAND.

1797 TO 1798.

WHEN Sir Ralph returned from the West Indies in 1797, the condition of Ireland was engaging the most serious attention of the Government. The appointment of Lord Fitzwilliam, in December 1794, to the situation of Lord Lieutenant, had raised the hopes of the Roman Catholics, which were defeated by his recall in 1795. The disappointment of their hopes had produced discontent, and, as was alleged, the severity of the Government, and the license of the Army, had led to disaffection, to a desire for separation from England, and to a traitorous correspondence with France.

It is not necessary to investigate minutely the truth of these allegations, but it may be remarked that when Doctor M'Nevin was examined before the Secret Committee of the House of Commons, in the year 1798, he was asked by Lord Castlereagh whether the measures of the Government complained of were not subsequent to various proceedings of the United Irishmen; he replied, that if his Lordship desired it, he was prepared to prove, by a comparison of dates, that the Government had throughout been the aggressors. It is to be lamented that Lord Castlereagh did not accept a challenge which might have established the truth by so simple a process as a comparison of dates. It must be admitted, on the one hand, that disaffection did exist, and, on the other, it cannot be denied that undue severity on the part of the Government, and uncontrolled license on the part of the Army, had a direct tendency to stimulate the exertions and to strengthen the hands of the disaffected. The feuds between the Protestants and Roman Catholics had assumed a very serious character. A battle had been fought at a village in the county of Armagh, called the "Diamond," in which the Catholics had been defeated. Orange lodges had been established, and persecution had been carried so far, that, in the month of December 1795, Lord Gosford, the Governor of the county of Armagh, had found it necessary to convene a meeting of the magistrates, to whom he stated, "That a persecution so ferocious was raging, that neither age nor sex, nor even acknowledged innocence were sufficient to excite mercy, much less to afford protection, and that the only crime with which the persecuted were charged, was simply a profession of the Roman Catholic faith." The defenders of this system, who included in their ranks the discontented and the disaffected, were not idle. In the autumn and winter of 1795, they appeared in arms, attacked houses and plundered them of arms, fired at magistrates, and assassinated witnesses, so that the country was exposed to the evils of civil war. Lord Carhampton was sent to the West to suppress the rioters, and he preceded the judges with his troops, opening the gaols as he went, and, without any form of trial, or any other authority than his own order, he sent the prisoners on board a tender, which sailed along the coast to receive them, and they were transferred to the service of the Navy. Such a precedent for superseding the authority of the Law, was promptly followed by magistrates and others, the Army was misled and disorganized, and misrule prevailed. Parliament was compelled to interfere, first to arrest the progress of actions which had been brought in the civil courts against those who had acted without authority from the Law, and ultimately it became necessary to pass a bill of indemnity.

The Irish Parliament met early in the month of

January 1796. A bill was passed enabling magistrates to declare any county in a state of insurrection, to break open houses at any hour, to search for arms, to arrest and send on board the fleet any one whom they suspected, and to imprison any man whom they found out of his house between sunset and sunrise. This was a very dangerous delegation of powers to magistrates, who had so abused their authority that it had been found necessary to protect them by a bill of indemnity. However much it may be lamented and justly condemned, it cannot be surprising, that in a country distracted by religious persecution, by the suspension of the authority of the law, by the exercise of power intrusted to incapable and unworthy hands, and by the pressure of a licentious army, some were at last found who were disposed to look to foreign aid as the only escape from this disastrous misrule, and that the French Government were prompt to avail themselves of the domestic weakness of a formidable enemy. Mr. Wolfe Tone, who had fled from Ireland to America, went to France early in the year 1796. He was not, and he did not pretend to be, the authorized representative of any portion of his countrymen; but the French Government, influenced by his reports and opinions, were induced to fit out an armament, which sailed from Brest on the 15th of December of that year. The fleet consisted of seventeen sail of the line, thirteen frigates, having on board fifteen thousand troops, and a large supply of arms and other muniments of war. It reached Bantry in safety, but it was dispersed by boisterous and adverse winds, and compelled to return to Brest.

Lord Camden in his despatch to the Government, detailing the arrival and dispersion of the French fleet, praises the excellent spirit shown by the regular and militia forces, the zeal displayed by all classes, and dwells especially on the cordiality and kindness with which the troops were received and their movements facilitated by the poorest of the people, and concludes by saying,—" In short, the general good disposition throughout the south and the west was so prevalent, that, had the enemy landed, their hope of assistance from the inhabitants would have been disappointed." In the report of a secret committee presented to the House of Lords, there is a statement connected with this event which deserves attention. It is there declared that, in the month of November 1796, the Irish Directory were informed of the armament preparing at Brest, but they subsequently received a letter to which they attached credit, and on which they acted, stating that the projected expedition was postponed for some months, and, consequently, no steps were taken to prepare the people for the arrival of the French; and to that circumstance one of the Irish Directory ascribed the loyalty of the inhabitants when the French fleet arrived off Bantry, and he confessed that the people were loyal because they were left to themselves. Such a statement, confirmed by the active display of the loyalty of the inhabitants on a most trying occasion, gives great weight to the assertion of Dr. M'Nevin that the Government had been the aggressors. The people, when left to themselves, were patient and submissive, and if they had been considerately, humanely, and justly treated, their attachment and fidelity might have been secured, but the irritation produced by religious persecution and arbitrary laws harshly enforced, enabled the leaders of the disaffected to seduce the people, and to involve the country in the most disastrous calamities.

When the Irish Parliament met in 1797, an effort was made to induce the Government to reward the loyalty displayed by the people when the French appeared off the coast, by adopting a firm, but lenient and just policy, and a motion was made in the House of Commons to that effect, but was negatived by a majority of ninety to seven. This result was so discouraging that Mr. Grattan and his friends would probably have abstained from making any farther effort, if they had not felt that they might be considered as having deserted their duty to the country if they did not bring under the consideration of Parliament an overture for peace, which had been submitted to the Lord-Lieutenant. In the preceding month of December a meeting had been held at Belfast, at which Arthur O'Connor and others were appointed to prepare resolutions to be laid before the Lord-Lieutenant, which stated in substance that the public mind would be restored to tranquillity, and impending danger averted by such a reform as would secure to population and property their due weight without distinction on account of religious opinions. These resolutions were laid before the Lord-Lieutenant, but were followed by no result. There were not only plausible, but even strong reasons for believing that the authors of these resolutions would, at that time, have been glad to be extricated from the difficulties and dangers with which they were environed, if the Government could have been prevailed upon to accept their substance in a sincere spirit. This opinion was most distinctly avowed in a memorial delivered to Government by

Arthur O'Connor, Emmett, and Dr. M'Nevin; and Emmett subsequently, when under examination, stated that if reform had at that time been conceded, the Irish Directory were prepared to have sent a message to France, stating "that the differences between the Government and the people had been adjusted, and dissuading them from attempting a second invasion of Ireland." Mr. Grattan and his friends declined to have any meeting, or to act in concert with the authors of the resolutions, but Mr. Ponsonby, with a view to the restoration of tranquillity, order, and legal government, proposed in Parliament such a plan of reform as he thought might have been safely adopted. The motion was rejected by 117 to 30. It is impossible to read the speeches of Mr. Grattan, on occasions so deeply affecting the fate of his country, without the greatest admiration of the calmness, the patriotism, and the wisdom with which they were inspired, and which were so characteristic of that virtuous and eminent statesman. Lord Castlereagh, indeed, commended the tone and temper with which Mr. Grattan had conducted these discussions, but he rejected his advice, and adopted a still more severe and irritating policy.

The first prominent act of the Government that

followed this discussion was a proclamation issued by General Lake, who commanded in the north, in which he stated "that it had become necessary to interpose with the King's troops, and that he had received authority and directions to act in such manner as the public safety required." The Law and the Constitution being thus superseded, Mr. Grattan lost no time in asking Mr. Pelham, the Secretary, whether the proclamation had been issued by his authority. Mr. Pelham declined to avow the proclamation, on which Mr. Grattan gave notice that he should move for it on the following day, but was prevented from doing so by the absence of the Ministers. The Lord-Lieutenant was, in the meanwhile, induced to send a message to Parliament acknowledging that the proclamation had been issued by his authority. This transaction is characteristic of the feebleness of the moderate, and of the ascendency of the violent party, which marked the whole course of Lord Camden's administration in Ireland.

The proclamation was admitted to have been illegal, but was justified on the ground of necessity. The inevitable consequence of such a defence was that the civil power was superseded by military authority, which was not only enforced, but very speedily abused. Acts of injustice and cruelty were daily perpetrated, the soldiers were debauched, and military discipline was injuriously relaxed. Addresses were presented to the King from the city of Dublin, and the counties of Antrim and Armagh, describing, in the strongest language, the sufferings of the people from the enforcement of military law, and from religious persecution. Such addresses were displeasing to the Government, and a proclamation was issued prohibiting all persons from meeting in unusual numbers, and Mr. Pelham intimated to the High Sheriffs of Kildare and the King's County, that a meeting of the inhabitants would not be permitted, and that the Lord-Lieutenant would direct the troops to prevent such assemblages. The counties that had intended to meet for the purpose of laying before the King the wrongs and injuries of which they complained, abandoned their purpose. In the month of April the Government received private information, which enabled them to arrest the persons and seize the papers of two committees of the Society of United Irishmen. These papers disclosed the origin, progress, and present means of that Society, and they also proved that it had been first established in 1791, by persons who were in no respect distinguished for education, ability, or influence, but who had made converts and gained strength under the pressure of coercive laws. None of those who were arrested, in consequence of the discovery of these papers, were Roman Catholics.

In the month of November 1797, Lord Carhampton had resigned the command of the Army in Ireland. This event, which was unexpected by the public, gave occasion for many conjectures. When it was known that Sir Ralph Abercromby had been selected to succeed to the command, those who believed that he would not tolerate the licentious proceedings of the Army, regarded his appointment as a proof that the English Government had begun to distrust the Irish policy, under which, disaffection, so far from having been suppressed, had increased and extended. Others supposed that the expectation of another attempt by the French to invade Ireland had suggested the necessity of placing the Army under the command of an officer of experience and ability. Probably both these reasons had some influence on the decision of the English Government.

These preliminary remarks on the state of Ireland under the administration of Lord Camden, were indispensable to show the difficulties with which Sir Ralph had to contend when he assumed the command of the Army in that country. It would have been easy to have proved the sufferings of the people and the disorganization of the Army, by extracts from an overwhelming mass of evidence; but enough has been said to indicate with clearness the naturally patient and submissive character of the people, the progress and causes of disaffection, the subversion of the civil authority, the abuse of military power, and the consequent disorganization of the Army. The difficulties inseparable from the command of the Army in a country so distracted and misgoverned, were greatly increased by the urgent necessity for promptly restoring discipline and efficiency to troops that might suddenly be called upon to meet an enemy in the field.

Sir Ralph had passed much time in Ireland, and he was too close an observer not to have studied the character and investigated the social and political condition of the people. He took great interest in the fortunes and fate of Ireland, and he expressed his opinions without reserve. His estimate of the people led him to appreciate justly the liveliness of their parts, and the levity which exposed them to the danger of being misguided by able and artful demagogues; but, while he knew their vices, and the origin of them, he knew that there was in their character much of generosity and warmth of feeling, which made them acutely sensitive when they were treated considerately and kindly. He said they were what the Government chose to make them, and to this opinion he adhered after the close of his command in Ireland. He knew from experience that the Irish made excellent soldiers when they were well commanded, and it had been remarked that he had very frequently intrusted the execution of critical service to regiments composed of Irishmen. His judgment of the upper classes of society, and of the purity and wisdom of the Government, was less favourable. He saw that the gentry were imperfectly educated; that they were devoted to the pursuits of pleasure and of political intrigue; and that they were ignorant or neglectful of the duties imposed on them as landlords, and as the friends and protectors of those who depended on them for their existence. He saw that the acts of the Government and of the Legislature were not regulated by respect for principle, which was the more to be lamented, as they were not controlled by the influence of an intelligent public opinion. Such were the opinions which Sir Ralph had formed during his preceding residence in Ireland, but he was quite prepared for the change which had been effected by the violence of the Government, the license of the Army, the seduction of the demagogues, and by the irritation arising from the sufferings of the people. So much was Sir Ralph under the influence of these considerations, and of the difficulties which might arise from a conflict between his own principles and those on which the Government acted, that after his appointment, but before he left London, he intimated to Mr. Pitt through Mr. Dundas, that if his measures were not approved he would willingly resign; and that if it should then be considered desirable to unite the offices of Lord-Lieutenant and Commander of the Forces in the person of Lord Cornwallis, he would be ready to serve under him. This was a very sincere offer on the part of Sir Ralph, as he had the highest esteem for Lord Cornwallis, with whom he lived on intimate terms, and he thought that their united and cordial efforts might be the means of restoring peace to Ireland.

In accepting the command in Ireland, under circumstances of so much difficulty, Sir Ralph felt that his first and most pressing duty was to exercise such control over the Army as would enable him to restore discipline, and to prepare for a struggle with the French if they should attempt another invasion. A very short residence in Dublin sufficed to convince him that an effort to restore discipline and to correct abuses in the Army, would be entirely thwarted by the powerful influence of the magistracy and gentry, and would be feebly, if at all, supported by the Government.

Sir Ralph arrived in Dublin on one of the early days of December 1797, and immediately proceeded to make such arrangements as appeared to him to be necessary for the defence of the country against the attack of a foreign enemy, and to restore the discipline of the Army. Efforts were very early made to induce the Government to counteract or resist the measures proposed by Sir Ralph for the safety of the country, but by his firmness he overcame them. The real struggle was with respect to the control, the distribution, and the employment of the Army. Sir Ralph wished and intended to concentrate the troops in large bodies, so that discipline might be enforced, and that they might be made fit to cope with the enemy in the field, and that on those occasions when their aid was required for the maintenance of domestic tranquillity they should act as the supporters and under the authority of the civil power. On the other hand, the magistrates and resident proprietors, who shrunk from the performance of their own duty, were unceasingly urging that the troops should at their call be dispersed and scattered through the country in small parties, under the pretence of securing their personal safety, but really for the purpose of enabling them to harass and oppress the people. They were strenuously supported by the principal advisers of the Lord-Lieutenant, which led to a singular struggle, in which a military commander wished to restrain the license of the troops, to protect the people, and to place the Army in subjection to the constitutional control of the civil power; while the Government and the magistrates encouraged and promoted the licentiousness of the troops, disregarded the authority of the law, and licensed the oppression of the people. The views and principles of the commander, who was the advocate of order, of justice, and of law, were enforced by him as affording the best chance of avoiding a rebellion, which was the inevitable consequence of the policy which finally prevailed.

The instructions which Sir Ralph issued very shortly after his arrival in Dublin, to the general officers under his command, place in the clearest light the principles on which he was resolved to act. These instructions state—" It is unnecessary to point out to the general officers the urgent necessity of preparing for any emergency that may arise in this country; their own observations must have convinced them that we may be called into the field without any previous notice."

Detailed and important instructions are then given for the improvement of discipline, the training and practice of the troops, and for the conduct of the generals. "In this country," it is stated, "it too frequently happens that the troops are called upon in aid of the civil magistrates, to support the peace of the country. Although on all occasions they ought to behave with firmness, yet they must not forget that they are only called upon to support the laws of the land, and not to step beyond the bounds of them. Any outrage or excess, therefore, on their part is highly culpable, and they are strictly enjoined to observe the greatest moderation and the strictest discipline when they are called upon to execute this part of their duty. Even in time of actual war, amongst all civilized nations, it is considered as disgraceful and subversive of all discipline, if soldiers are allowed to be licentious."

On the important point of internal defence, the instructions are to this effect:—" The internal defence of the country in its present circumstances, will require the attention of the general officers. It will be impossible to leave the well-disposed inhabitants totally unprotected in case the troops are withdrawn. They will therefore turn this matter seriously in their minds, and make such arrangements as this object may require. It is recommended to the general officers, to have a confidential correspondence with the heads of the Yeomanry corps in their different districts, on whom the internal tranquillity of the country must in a great measure depend. The general officers will give these gentlemen such advice, instructions, and support as the local situation of the country may require, to enable them to preserve tranquillity, and to prevent insurrections, or the excesses of the banditti which may show themselves in any part of the country, and which must happen, unless they will exert with vigour and energy the means they have in their power to prevent it. Should any insurrection arise in the country requiring the interposition of the troops, they are to be ordered to march in such force as will be sufficient to quell it instantly, as it is always attended with bad consequences, where troops receive any check in the first instance."

These instructions indicate with distinctness the view which Sir Ralph took of the trust which had been confided to him, and the means by which he proposed to perform it. From these principles he never swerved, and he preferred the resignation of his important command to any concession which he would have deemed inconsistent with his duty to the public. While Sir Ralph had firmly resolved on the course of conduct which it was his duty to follow, he acted in a temperate and conciliatory spirit, wishing to carry with him the opinion and judgment of those who were bound to yield obedience to his authority. Writing on the 13th of December 1797 to General Lake, who commanded in the north, and who, as has been stated, had issued a proclamation under the authority of the Lord-Lieutenant, superseding the Law and the Constitution, Sir Ralph says, "The very dispersed state of the troops in the northern district naturally attracted my attention. I know how difficult it is for the Government of this country to resist the applications of individuals for protection, and perhaps in some cases they ought not to be resisted. I am convinced, however, of the absolute necessity of contracting to a *certain degree*, the quarters of the troops under your command. In their present state they are exposed to be corrupted, to be disarmed and made prisoners. When wanted they cannot be easily assembled, and if called away suddenly, a general dismay would take place in the country. You will therefore take such measures for bringing the troops more together, as you shall judge expedient."

When General Lake read this letter, he must have seen that the system was changed, but he could not fail to feel, that it had been announced to him with delicacy, and with due respect for the peculiar position in which he was placed.

However highly Sir Ralph had estimated beforehand the difficulties with which he should have to contend in his command in Ireland, he speedily found that they were more serious than he had anticipated. When he arrived in Dublin he naturally fell into the society of the higher classes, and of those who were closely connected with the Government by official and other ties. Their conversation betrayed such unrelenting hostility to the people, such an ardent desire for the most severe measures, unrestrained by law and the authority of the civil power, that Sir Ralph was compelled to abandon all mixed society, and to devote himself to the firm and calm maintenance of that policy which his duty to his country prescribed. It would be a mistake to undervalue the importance of such conversation, for it had been the great misfortune of Ireland, that it had never been under the control of an intelligent public opinion; and the consequence had been, that the tone of the higher classes of society in Dublin had not only indicated the tendency, but had exercised the most powerful influence over the policy of the Government.

After a lapse of more than a quarter of the present century, it happened that the writer of this Memoir was asked by one of the most observing and sensible statesmen who has filled the office of Chief Secretary in Ireland, to give him the character of a lawyer, who had been selected to occupy the high station of Lord Chancellor. The request was complied with, and afterwards he was told by the Secretary, that the character given was in all respects just, except that it omitted one of the greatest merits of the new Chancellor, that he was proof against the flattery and seductions of the aristocratic society, which misled and corrupted all the Englishmen who were sent to govern Ireland. It is not surprising, therefore, that the views and opinions of Sir Ralph were as displeasing to the Government as to the aristocratic class of society.

The interference of the Government, and the difficulties thrown in his way, compelled Sir Ralph to address the following letter to Mr. Elliot, dated on the 25th December, the month in which he arrived in Dublin :—

"Mr. Pelham, before he went to England, desired me to communicate with you in the same manner as if he were present, and, from the confidential situation in which you are placed, I naturally address myself to you on any occasion of moment. When I was asked to take the command of the Army in Ireland, I then stated the objections which the nature of the Government of this country suggested to my mind, and I then felt the delicacy of my situation. I was then assured by those with whom I communicated, that I should labour under no difficulty or restraint in my command, and, from the conversations I held with those well acquainted with the government of Ireland, I had reason to expect that in time of war the Army would be totally under my command, the patronage of it excepted; and I was taught to believe that my recommendation of deserving officers would be sufficient to entitle them to promotion. From the experience I have had since my arrival in this country, and from looking forward to future consequences, I find it indispensable for the good of the King's service, and to prevent any future embarrassments, that there should be a free and explicit explanation on this subject. A divided command in the direction of an Army is perfectly incompatible with those principles by which military affairs are guided. It is, therefore, necessary that the Lord-Lieutenant should take the sole command, and the senior officer in Ireland act as his Lieutenant-General; or that he should delegate it to the Commander-in-Chief appointed by his Majesty. I can see no other alternative. If this line is not drawn, delays must for ever arise from a divided command; from a diffidence proceeding from an undefined situation; from the interference of office, and the appeal of Boards from the Commander-in-Chief to the Lord-Lieutenant. In times such as the present, such obstructions to the public service cannot be permitted to arise. With the highest respect for the situation and character of his Excellency the Lord-Lieutenant, I request a clear decision on this point. I came here from no motive of emolument, and I may say of ambition, except that of being useful, as far as my abilities went; and it is my earnest wish not to quit a station in which I have been placed. I trust to receive through you such an explanation as will settle this point."

This plain and explicit letter was met by verbal and unsatisfactory assurances, so that there was no alternative but to persevere, and to wait until some tangible and decisive event should arise.

The Duke of York, the Commander-in-Chief of the Army, who was warmly and most faithfully attached to Sir Ralph, desired that he would communicate to him the opinion he formed of the condition of the country and the Army, and would keep him informed of all his material proceedings in Ireland. In compliance with the wish of the Duke of York, Sir Ralph, on the 28th December, addressed a letter to his Royal Highness, from which the following and only material extracts are made:—

"The disturbances which have arisen in the south are exactly similar to those which have always prevailed in that part of the country, and they hold out the old grievances of tithes and oppressive rents. The country gentlemen and magistrates do not do their duty; they are timid and distrustful, and ruin the troops by calling on them upon every occasion to execute the law, and to afford them personal protection."

After giving details with respect to the composition and discipline of the Army, Sir Ralph goes on to state:—

"With an army composed of so various a description of troops, and in a country so unprepared for war, it requires all the authority that the Lord-Lieutenant can give me, to enable me to carry on the King's service. I have no reason to say that Lord Camden has refused me his support, but the difficulties and delays I experience will render my situation irksome and my labour unavailing. I have the honour to enclose a copy of a letter which I have written on this subject, to which I have only received general and verbal answers. I am determined, however, to act with firmness and prudence, and to exercise that command over the Army which the situation of this country and the public welfare require."

In the month of January, Sir Ralph visited the south of Ireland, and, on the 23d, he wrote to Lord Camden from Cork :—

" I have the satisfaction to assure your Excellency that, as far as my information goes, the country through which I have passed is in a state of tranquillity. Of this I have had the fullest assurance from every gentleman with whom I have conversed. It would now be very desirable if the troops could, without alarming the gentlemen, be collected, and their discipline restored, which suffers exceedingly from their dispersed state. I am morally certain that many of the regiments could not, at present, take the field from their various wants, which cannot be known or supplied till more brought together. The yeomanry appear to advantage; they are well clothed and mounted, and express great willingness and zeal. I am, however, nearly convinced that to bring them together, and to appoint officers to command them, must not be attempted. They must be left at home, and appointed for the defence of the interior."

On the same day Sir Ralph wrote to Mr. Pelham :—

"The dispersed state of the troops is really ruinous to the service. The best regiments in Europe could not long stand such usage. The real state of the country can alone determine the necessity for it. If I could be informed what number of regiments in aid of the yeomanry would be wanted in each province for the preservation of the peace of the country, I would willingly abandon a certain proportion for that peculiar purpose, provided the remainder were to be kept together, and in a situation to move if a foreign enemy should appear. I have found the cavalry, in general, unfit for service, and more than one-half of the infantry dispersed over the face of the country, in general under officers very little able to command them. At Fermoy more than three-fourths of the light infantry are 'on command.'"

During his visit to the south, Sir Ralph did not fail to examine with care all the points at which the landing of the French might be expected, and such preparations for defence as had been made were found to be in a most defective condition. The tranquillity of the south, as described by Sir Ralph, in the first month of the year in which the Rebellion broke out, is a striking fact. The temper and earnestness with which he enforces the necessity of concentrating the troops, in order that discipline may be restored and an army formed, capable of opposing a foreign foe, who might at any moment appear, ought to have engaged the serious attention and to have secured the cordial support of Government.

It is to be observed that Sir Ralph, in his communications with Government, speaks in general terms of the relaxed discipline of the Army, and abstains from all allusion to the excesses committed by the troops, when they were called out, to calm the fears, or gratify the resentment of a timid and jealous magistracy. Assuredly this did not proceed from indifference to the cruelty and injurious consequences of such conduct, but from his honest desire to counteract the evil, by leading the Government to consent to the concentration of the troops, and to the use of the civil power, aided, when necessary, by the yeomanry, as the means of preserving internal peace. The exclusive object of Sir Ralph was to obtain such control over the Army as would enable him to make it efficient for the defence of the country, and he therefore carefully abstained, as far as possible, from criticism on the past, and shunned whatever could give countenance to the suspicion that he was acting from party or political bias.

When the principles on which he was acting came to be understood, he received overtures of support from persons of influence and character, who approved of his course; but he courteously rejected them, as inconsistent with the position which he had taken, and with his resolution to rest his character on the purity of his purpose and the soundness of his views. The principles on which Sir Ralph was resolved to act in the performance of his duty to the public, in a season of difficulty and danger, having been distinctly and unreservedly communicated to the Government, he was fully justified in expecting either to have received cordial support, or to have been frankly told that his views were inconsistent with those of the advisers of the Lord-Lieutenant, and that they could not be sanctioned. So far from this being the case, the course pursued by Lord Camden was as embarrassing to Sir Ralph as it was unfortunate for his own character, and the welfare of the country which he governed. In their personal intercourse, Lord Camden was not only courteous but kind, and when Sir Ralph reasoned with him, his judgment seemed to be convinced, and at the close of their conversations he repeatedly said, "Now I must go to *my* friends and hear very different opinions." Lord Camden was, in truth, the victim of the passions and violence of his advisers; he had good intentions, but was of infirm purpose, and did not possess the courage to assert or even to assist what he felt to be right. Sir Ralph was touched by his amiable qualities, and by his personal kindness, but he could not respect Lord Camden as a public man; he felt for him, as holding a position to which he was unequal, and regarded his errors and faults rather with compassion than with resentment. From the aristocratic and Protestant oligarchy, who were the real rulers of the country, Sir Ralph met with no mercy. All his acts were grossly misrepresented, the most bitter abuse was heaped upon him, and his conduct was attributed to the falsest motives. The patriotic Lord Charlemont, writing to his friend Dr. Haliday, in the month of February, warmly commends the conduct of Sir Ralph, who, he says, "has acted with the strictest propriety in his most difficult situation, and has the happiness of being cordially disliked and abused."

Such a state of affairs was not calculated for long endurance. It would be tedious and useless to give the details of the many instances in which the measures of Sir Ralph were interfered with or thwarted. One or two cases may be selected to show the steadiness with which he endeavoured to restore the ascendency of the civil authority, and to restrain the excesses of the Army. In writing to Mr. Secretary Pelham, on the case of a serjeant of a Fencible regiment who had been murdered by the people, a crime which was followed by great excesses on the part of the troops, Sir Ralph says—
"It is much to be regretted that the civil magistrate has not hitherto discovered the murderer of the serjeant, and I still more lament that no evidence has been brought forward sufficient to convict the authors of the notorious acts of violence which have been, in some measure, the consequence of the murder. It is to be hoped, Sir, that the magistrates of the county of Kildare will be instructed to prosecute still farther the investigation

of this business. Although they may not discover the murderer of the serjeant, they cannot fail to discover the soldiers who first set fire to the houses, and committed several acts of violence at noonday, and in face of all the inhabitants of Newbridge. The soldiers are all at Kildare, and every assistance shall be afforded in the farther prosecution of the inquiry. The future discipline of the Army may depend on the conduct observed in this affair. If the civil power should decline taking any farther steps, it must be taken up in a different point of view." This letter supplies the strongest practical proof of the soundness and sufficiency of the means by which Sir Ralph proposed to restore the discipline of the Army, to re-establish the ascendency of the civil power, and to protect the people from the licentious excesses of the troops.

In writing to General Johnstone, who commanded at Fermoy, Sir Ralph says:—"I regret the death of Mr. St. George and Mr. Uniacke; your exertions in assisting the civil magistrate in apprehending the perpetrators of a horrid murder are highly commendable, and promise to be the means of eventually bringing them to public justice. I have always wished that the law should be supported by the troops when called on properly, but I have as strongly wished that they should not take any part that was not strictly legal, because when we once depart from that rule we subject ourselves to much inconvenience. I hope the magistrates have not put their intention of burning houses in force. I hope the soldiers have taken no part in it."

Sir Ralph again develops his views in a letter which he addressed to the Duke of York on the 17th February, after his tour in the south :—" I can say with satisfaction that in the country through which I passed, I found the people quiet. That dissatisfaction and disaffection prevail cannot be doubted or denied; it requires a watchful eye to preserve the internal tranquillity of this country. It is very unfortunate that the upper orders of men have fallen, in general, into a state of despondency, and seem to have given up the cause. To rouse them, and to call forth their exertions, ought to be the great object of the Government. On this principle, I have endeavoured as far as possible to resist the interference of the troops in all matters where the civil magistrate ought alone to have interfered. I clearly saw that the discipline of the troops would be completely ruined, and that they would be led into a thousand irregularities contrary to law, which would bring disgrace upon themselves, and in which they ought not to be supported by the Government of the country. I flatter myself that the effect of this will be to force the gentlemen to exert themselves, and to trust to the yeomanry, on whom they must ultimately rely for their internal security in case the troops should be called to act against a foreign enemy. On no occasion, however, which has been really urgent, have I objected to the troops being employed, guarding them at the same time against any excess in the execution of their duty."

These extracts, which might be greatly multiplied, sufficiently confirm the assertion by which they have been preceded, that throughout the struggle between Lord Camden's advisers and Sir Ralph, the commander of the Army was the steady and consistent vindicator of the authority of the civil power, and the protector of the people, while the Government were the zealous and successful advocates of military rule, and of the uncontrolled license of the troops.

On the 26th of February, Sir Ralph issued the following celebrated order :—" The very disgraceful frequency of courts-martial, and the many complaints of irregularities in the conduct of the troops in this kingdom, having too unfortunately proved the Army to be in a state of licentiousness which must render it formidable to every one but the enemy, the Commander-in-Chief thinks it necessary to demand from all Generals commanding districts and brigades, as well as commanding officers of regiments, that they exert for themselves, and compel from all officers under their command, the strictest and most unremitting attention to the discipline, good order, and conduct of their men, such as may restore the high and distinguished reputation which the British troops have been accustomed to enjoy in every part of the world. It becomes necessary to recur, and most pointedly to attend to the standing orders of the kingdom, which, at the same time that they direct military assistance to be given at the requisition of the civil magistrate, positively forbid the troops to act (but in case of attack) without his presence and authority, and the most clear and positive orders are to be given to the officers commanding the party for this purpose."

That Sir Ralph was fully justified in believing himself authorized to announce the principles on which he was resolved to control and regulate the conduct of the Army, is apparent from a letter which Lord Camden addressed to the Duke of Portland, two days before the order was issued. After some remarks on Sir Ralph's report as to the military defence of the south, the Lord-Lieutenant proceeds :—

"But your Grace is not to imagine, that Sir Ralph Abercromby has failed to turn his mind to the internal defence of the country. He has considered it, as he does every subject which occurs to him, gravely and deeply, and I have had frequent conversations with him upon it. He is impressed, as every man who resides in this country must be, with the extent and danger of that conspiracy which exists, and of the necessity of watching and attending to it most closely. He is, at the same time, much impressed with the necessity of drawing the Army into larger bodies, with a view to resist invasion; and he is of opinion that steps should be taken for that purpose, and to give opportunity to the gentlemen of the country to feel their own strength, to ascertain the capacity of their own exertions, and the credit which ought to be given to the services of the Yeomanry corps. I so *perfectly* agree with Sir Ralph in the propriety of this measure, that I lost no time in communicating with several gentlemen connected with various parts of the country, who feel the justice of his remarks, and are so much inclined to adopt some of the suggestions he has made, that I propose very speedily to make some arrangements which will disengage the army from part of the duty that is now imposed upon them in various parts of the kingdom. I am desirous to take this opportunity of expressing the very high satisfaction I have received from his Majesty's gracious compliance with my representations in appointing a Commander-in-Chief of Sir Ralph Abercromby's experience, and I am convinced the selection of this very able officer will be of the most essential advantage to his Majesty's service, as in his instance, the greatest military experience is combined with remarkably good sense and knowledge of the world."

This letter proves how clearly Lord Camden understood the principles on which Sir Ralph was resolved to act, and how perfectly he agreed in their propriety and wisdom. There cannot be a doubt, that if Lord Camden had adhered to the opinions expressed in this letter, he would have been cordially supported by the English Government. Unfortunately for his own fame and the peace of Ireland, he displayed neither the courage nor the virtue to act on the principles in which he agreed, or to resist the importunity and violence of his intemperate and reckless advisers. All discussion of Irish policy has here been avoided, except in so far as it was necessary to illustrate the personal conduct of Sir Ralph, but it is impossible not to feel, that if Lord Camden had steadily adhered to, and acted upon the view which he had imbibed from the Commander-in-Chief, there was still a reasonable chance that the rebellion might have been prevented.

After issuing the order of the 26th February, Sir Ralph went to inspect the Army in the north. The advisers of Lord Camden were alarmed and exasperated by the firm and judicious conduct of Sir Ralph, which they felt was beginning to make a serious impression, and they availed themselves of his absence to weaken his influence with the Lord-Lieutenant, and to instil into the minds of the militia officers, that the statements contained in the order were an insult to the character of their corps. It also happened, that at this time, Lord Moira took his seat in the Irish House of Lords, and made a motion, in which he described the distracted state of the country, and in which, as of necessity, he dwelt on the excesses committed by the troops. The enemies of Sir Ralph seized upon this event, and as unscrupulously as falsely, asserted that his conduct was prompted by a desire to promote a political intrigue, and that he was acting in concert with Lord Moira. On his return from the north

Sir Ralph found the storm thus raised violently raging, and he wrote to Colonel Brownrigg, then Secretary to the Duke of York, that the Lord-Lieutenant had candidly imparted to him, that his order of the 26th February had been taken up as a political manœuvre in conjunction with Lord Moira, and he then adds: " Lord Moira is but little known to me, his politics have certainly never allured me, and the profession of a politician I have never followed. Independence has always had too powerful an attraction to allow me to engage with any set of men. I came here determined not to regard trifling inconveniences, and to struggle with more serious difficulties, but if I am to have a powerful host to contend with, I do not see how I am to keep my ground."

Having thus prepared the Duke of York for the resignation of his command, Sir Ralph waited on the Lord-Lieutenant, and presented to him the following letter: " Understanding from your Excellency's communication yesterday that the orders issued on the 26th of February last had been construed as a political manœuvre, permit me to lay before your Excellency, with candour and truth, what has passed in my mind and influenced my conduct since I took the command of his Majesty's troops in this kingdom. I have lamented the general alienation of the minds of the people from the Government. I have regretted the supineness and the despondency of individuals, and I have seen, with anxious concern, the loose texture of the Irish army, and their relaxed discipline. Under these circumstances, it did not become me to remain neuter or inactive. It has been my study to acquire some knowledge of the country. Several important military arrangements have been recommended and carried into execution. I have personally, as well as by orders which I have issued, endeavoured to correct abuses, and to support a stricter discipline; and I have, as far as became me, stimulated the exertions of the country, by pointing out the necessity of calling out part of the Yeomanry in case the troops should be called away to face a foreign enemy; and I have procured arms to be sent to the different parts of the kingdom, to be put into the hands of the well-affected in case of necessity. The orders of the 26th February were issued expressly for this purpose, and the whole spirit and tenor of them tend to that end. I acknowledge that I did not consider the proclamation of the 18th May last as then in force; at the same time, I am clearly of opinion that the interpretation and execution of it could not have been left to officers of all descriptions without great inconvenience, and even danger.

"I beg leave to assure your Excellency that I never was a political man; that I have no political connexion with the noble Lord who was lately in this kingdom, and but a very slight personal one. Previously to my coming to Ireland, I had no communication with any of his Majesty's Ministers on the state of the country. After my appointment, I communicated to Mr. Pitt, through Mr. Dundas, that if I did not meet the public mind, I should most willingly resign, or serve under a superior officer with whom I knew that I could act. I now renew to your Excellency what I then expressed, being perfectly convinced of the necessity of it, because, if I do not possess the confidence of those with whom your Excellency advises, I must impede the operations of your Government."

Lord Camden was thus driven to make his election between the firm, humane, and constitutional policy of Sir Ralph, in which he had expressed his agreement in his letter to the Duke of Portland, and the advice of those who did not scruple to avow their anxious wish that the people should be forced into a rebellion, from the suppression of which they anticipated a gratifying triumph. Lord Camden took the course which was consistent with the infirmity of his character; he wished to retain Sir Ralph, but he had not the manliness to give him that support which was essential to the maintenance of his authority and his system.

After the delay of a week, Lord Camden replied to Sir Ralph's letter. The Lord-Lieutenant cordially absolved Sir Ralph from the imputation of having participated in a political manœuvre, and expressed his agreement with most of the important parts of Sir Ralph's letter, but he adds : " At the same time, you have had the candour to acknowledge that you did not consider the proclamation of the 18th May as then in force. There is no doubt that until such a proclamation is recalled, or until the state of the country is so altered that it is a dead letter, the proclamation exists. Under that proclamation, the military received orders to act without waiting for the civil magistrate. A responsibility is thrown upon the Army, which is unpleasant to him who commands it, and upon the officer who may be called upon to exert himself individually; and although I may lament the necessity, that necessity exists, and since it does exist, it appears to me that the proclamation must be acted upon. I therefore look with confidence to some explanation of that part of your orders which you issued under the impression that the proclamation was not in force, to determine whether it will be most agreeable to you to make such alteration yourself, or whether you would be desirous to receive an intimation to that effect from me."

Lord Camden then assures Sir Ralph that he does possess the confidence of those with whom he advises, and also of the English Government, who are impressed with the incalculable evils, both in a military and a political view, which would follow from his resignation. The delay which took place in replying to Sir Ralph's letter, in which he had intimated the necessity of his resigning his situation, is easily accounted for by the struggle which must have arisen in the mind of Lord Camden in deciding between the approval of the policy of Sir Ralph, which he had expressed to the Duke of Portland, and the advice of those with whom he consulted.

The advisers of Lord Camden had prevailed, and the difference between him and Sir Ralph had now assumed a distinct and decisive shape. Lord Camden insisted that the troops should be authorized to act without the intervention of the civil power, and that the proclamation of the 18th May, authorizing them so to act, should be enforced. Sir Ralph, on the contrary, contended that the interpretation of the proclamation could not be left to officers without great inconvenience and danger, without ruining the discipline of the Army, and without leading to excesses oppressive to the people.

Sir Ralph did not hesitate for a moment as to the course which it was his duty to pursue. On the same day on which Lord Camden's reply reached him, he wrote to Mr. Secretary Dundas, to acquaint him, that the breach between him and the advisers of the Lord-Lieutenant made it impossible that he should retain his command; and he expresses an earnest wish that his removal might be so ordered as to give the least possible interruption to the military business in so distracted a country, and the least handle for speculation. Sir Ralph, justly appreciating the influence which had directed the conduct of the Lord-Lieutenant, thus expresses himself in his reply to Lord Camden—" I am sensible, my Lord, that there never was a time when private concerns or private opinions ought less to influence all who are in the service of the public; yet, my Lord, there is one point on which no man who is fit for public employment can be indifferent. No man can be indifferent to his own character. He cannot trust it in the hands of those who have endeavoured to deprive him of it. Were I to remain under your Excellency's orders, I should feel diffidence and distrust from the experience which I have had of the past conduct of those with whom your Excellency advises, which would render me very unfit for the command in such a time as the present. I, therefore, entreat you will be pleased to move his Majesty graciously to permit me to resign my situation, in which I cannot be continued with advantage to his service."

Lord Camden made another effort to retain Sir Ralph, and offered to act as a mediator, and to remove the impressions which his conduct had made on others. To this offer Sir Ralph replied on the 27th March:—" I cannot admit that any part of my conduct requires any interposition to give a favourable construction to it, or to remove any impressions which that conduct has occasioned. While your goodness in these particulars is an additional motive for gratitude, it is likewise a proof that it would be improper in me to remain in a situation in which my conduct could only be supported by your personal authority, and not by the opinion of those around you."

In the meanwhile, the English Government were

not inactive. Mr. Dundas, in his own name, and in that of his colleagues, urged Sir Ralph to make every possible concession, so that he might retain a command in which his services were so highly valued by them. Mr. Dundas also transmitted to Sir Ralph copies of the correspondence between Lord Camden and the Duke of Portland, in which Lord Camden expressed, in the warmest manner, his confidence in Sir Ralph; and the Duke of Portland stated, that there had never existed in England the remotest suspicion that Sir Ralph's conduct had been influenced by political motives; that all his colleagues, as well as the kingdom at large, did justice to the correctness of his manner of thinking, and to the uprightness of his conduct; and therefore he expressed an anxious hope that his discernment and his devotion to the public service, for which he had always been so eminently conspicuous, would induce him to continue in a situation which it was so necessary that he should retain. The only objection that ever was made in England to Sir Ralph's order was one which was not unnatural in those who were engaged in political warfare. They felt that the authoritative admission of the bad discipline and excesses of the Army gave an advantage to their opponents, and they felt this the more because they were convinced that it was true. If Sir Ralph had been supported, the scale would have been turned in favour of the Government, for the evil which was justly complained of would have been effectually redressed.

Sir Ralph was too well acquainted with the temper, the character, and the conduct of Lord Camden's advisers, to be moved by the flattering solicitations of the Duke of Portland and his colleagues.

Sir Ralph's final resolution was intimated in the following letter which he wrote to Mr. Dundas on the 24th of March :—

"I have the honour to acknowledge the receipt of your letters of the 18th and 20th March, with their enclosures. I trust that my letter of the 22d, which I wrote previous to the receipt of either of yours, will carry so much weight with it that you will believe that I am not actuated either by resentment or by caprice. I feel the most perfect conviction that the principal members of Lord Camden's cabinet have lost their confidence, if they ever had any, in me; that they did, during my absence, attempt my ruin by their machinations here and in England, is a matter beyond all doubt. It is perfectly impossible for me to act with them in future but with the greatest distrust, which, in these difficult times, must cramp every endeavour of mine to render any essential service, were I to remain here. I think you, who have long known me, will believe me when I assure you that I am no politician; and as to the particular construction put on my order, it was so unfounded, that when I gave that order I never had read either Lord Moira's speech or that of the Lord Chancellor; that I mentioned to Lord Camden my disapprobation of the mode of employing soldiers in this country, that I have told Mr. Pelham that the best troops in Europe would not stand such usage, are undoubted facts. The abuses and the insubordination of the Irish army called for the most strenuous exertions on my part, and the most positive orders. If I were to enter into any detail upon this subject, I think I could convince you, or any candid person, of the necessity of the steps I have taken, since I came to this country, to reform the Army, on which the salvation of this country must principally depend. I have nothing to charge my conscience with, and whatever is the consequence I cannot abate one single fact or sentiment I have now the honour of expressing to you."

The motives which governed the conduct of Sir Ralph on this important occasion, are very fully stated in the following letter which he addressed to his eldest son, for the information of his father, then in the ninety-fourth year of his age :—

"It is natural to suppose that my father should be anxious to know the true reason of my resignation. Be so good as to tell him in a few words, that the struggle has been, in the first place, whether I was to have the command of the Army really or nominally, and then whether the character and discipline of it were to be degraded and ruined in the mode of using it, either from the facility of one man, or from the violence and oppression of a set of men, who have for more than twelve months employed it in measures which they durst not avow or sanction. Lord Camden, in weakly yielding these points, has betrayed the situation of the Commander-in-Chief; has thrown the Army into the hands of a faction; has made it a tool under their direction; and has, I think, overset himself; for, although the British Government has prejudged me, they cannot but see the weakness and folly of all that has been done here. Within these twelve months, every crime, every cruelty that could be committed by Cossacks or Calmucks, has been transacted here.

"The words of the order of the 26th February were strong, the circumstances required it; it has not abated the commission of enormities, and I will venture to predict that when the moment for calling forth the Irish Army arrives, one-half of it will dissolve in a month. The proclamation, in the face of which the order alluded to was said to be, is given up both here and in England, and it is unnecessary to say anything on the subject. Within less than two months since the issuing of my orders, a private man has thrown a chair at the colonel of his regiment, when sent for to be reprimanded. Houses have been burned, men murdered, others half hanged; a young lady has been carried off by a detachment of dragoons, and in the room where she was an officer was shot through the thigh, and a blunderbuss snapped at another gentleman's head. These are but a few of the enormities which have disgraced us of late; were the whole to be collected, what a picture would it present!

"Such a degree of insubordination has been allowed, that the general officers write directly to the Castle, overlooking every decency and order. Almost all of those who were here before me have a plot or a conspiracy which they cherish, and which is the subject of their correspondence and consequence; and instead of attending to their duty, and to the discipline of their troops, they are either acting as politicians, or as justices of the peace, a situation which most of them have solicited. In short, I feel the greatest satisfaction in quitting a country where I have been betrayed. Of this I am certain, that there must be some change, otherwise the country will be lost. The late ridiculous farce acted by Lord Camden and his cabinet must strike every one. They have declared the kingdom in rebellion, when the orders of his Excellency might be carried over the whole kingdom by an orderly dragoon, or a writ executed without any difficulty, a few places in the mountains excepted. Lord Camden is a most virtuous man, and as far as personal civility goes, I am much indebted to him.

"DUBLIN CASTLE, *April* 23, 1798."

The reference in Sir Ralph's letters to the efforts that had been made to ruin his character in Ireland and England is illustrated by the following facts:—The advisers of Lord Camden took advantage of Sir Ralph's absence from Dublin to hold a meeting in the Speaker's room, at which they deliberately discussed and considered whether, with the greatest prospect of success, they could induce the House of Commons to pass a resolution that Sir Ralph had, by his conduct, proved himself to be an enemy to his country, or whether they should proceed at once by impeachment. The decision was in favour of the former course of proceeding.

A gentleman of family and fortune, who had formerly served in the same regiment with Sir Ralph, became acquainted with what was passing, and he forced himself into the room of Mr. Pelham, who was sick in bed, and communicated the fact to him. Mr. Pelham at once took such measures as effectually crushed the plot. The same advisers of the Lord-Lieutenant also induced a nobleman of high rank and great influence, to go to England for the purpose of impressing all those to whom he had access with the impolitic and dangerous course which Sir Ralph was pursuing. These facts, which were certain, were sufficient to justify the strong expressions of Sir Ralph, but they did not stand alone.

It is proper to insert the letter which Sir Ralph addressed to the Duke of York on his resignation, as it shows how carefully he abstained from saying anything that could create a prejudice against individuals, and how anxiously he limited his observations to the vindication of his own personal conduct. On the 27th of March, Sir Ralph writes to the Duke of York :—" Finding that my remaining in the command in this country can no longer be of any advantage to his Majesty's service, I have applied to the Lord-Lieutenant to move his Majesty that I may be permitted to resign my present situation. I feel the fullest conviction that every act of mine since I came to Ireland has proceeded from the most earnest regard for the good of his Majesty's service, that my whole attention has been directed to the care of the Army, and that I have not only avoided all personal connexion with political men, but every interference with their politics. I shall hope for an opportunity of convincing your Royal Highness and his Majesty that the construction put on my conduct is most unjust."

The following letter from Sir Ralph to the writer of this Memoir, and dated March 23, gives a more detailed account of the movement against him, which was conducted by the Speaker, Mr. Foster.

"You know the reluctance I had in accepting the command in this country; it was in obedience to the King's pleasure; and having accepted it, neither inconvenience nor serious difficulties would have induced me to quit it at this time. Since my arrival I have been under the necessity of supporting myself by great exertions and strong representations, otherwise I should have been a mere cipher, or what is worse, a tool in the hands of a party who govern this country. Their dislike to me has of course been visible, and in my absence they took the opportunity of attempting to crush me. The Speaker at the head of a junto met in his chamber, canvassed and censured my order, and, interfering in a matter which did not belong to them, sent a deputation to Mr. Pelham to convey to him their opinion, and their determination to bring it before Parliament. This was only part of their plan; they wrote the most furious representations against me to the Duke of Portland, and to others of high rank in England.

"This mode of proceeding was so precipitate and so hostile, that there can be no doubt of their intention to ruin me. After this there can be no mutual confidence. In times so difficult, it is next to impossible to separate the civil and military business of the country, and with all the wisdom, all the vigour that can be shown, it is impossible for any General to answer for success. Should, therefore, any one thing go wrong, I could expect nothing but the fullest effects of their resentment. I am not easily alarmed, but I cannot help feeling my situation, which, however, would not alone determine me, if I did not see that my remaining here would impede the King's service.

"Thus the matter stands. Now for the order.

"The abuses of all kinds I found here can scarcely be believed or enumerated. I tried various means with little success; it was necessary to speak out; the order is strong, but be assured it was necessary. The way in which the troops have been employed, would ruin the best in Europe. Here are 35,000 Yeomanry, raised for the express purpose of protecting the country. To them I have urged the necessity of applying for assistance, but in vain. I therefore restricted the troops to the standing orders of the kingdom, that their discipline might be pursued if possible, and that the gentlemen might be obliged to trust to the Yeomanry, on whom they must ultimately depend, in case the troops should be called away to oppose a foreign enemy."

From this time, Sir Ralph considered himself as only holding his command until the arrival of his successor, and as being absolved from all serious responsibility, by acting only under the orders of the Lord-Lieutenant. To remove all doubt as to the exact position in which he stood, and to vindicate his own consistency and character, Sir Ralph addressed the following note to all the general officers commanding districts in Ireland : " I think it is an attention due to myself to inform you, that I expect soon to be relieved in the command of his Majesty's troops in this kingdom."

The impression made by the conduct of Sir Ralph was such, that his enemies were restrained from exulting in their victory, by the consciousness that his resignation would be regarded by very many as a public misfortune. Notwithstanding the unjust treatment which Sir Ralph had experienced from the advisers of Lord Camden, he neither yielded to resentment, nor relaxed in such efforts as, under his circumstances, he could properly make, for the maintenance of discipline in the Army, or for the safety of the country. In his communications with the general officers, he did not fail to admonish them most earnestly to exercise the great powers which were intrusted to them by the Lord-Lieutenant's proclamation now to be enforced, with the greatest lenity, and to be cautious in exceeding the limits of the law. Deeply impressed with the inefficiency and disorganization of the Irish Army, and with the imminent probability of foreign invasion, Sir Ralph urgently pressed Lord Camden to apply for an additional force of disciplined troops, which must be drawn from England, as any attempt to raise them in Ireland would only be adding to the danger.

The unabated kindness, and the amiable qualities displayed by Lord Camden throughout these transactions, induced Sir Ralph to make a great sacrifice to aid him in the perplexities in which he was involved by the weakness of his character. In a letter to Mr. Dundas, Sir Ralph says, " If the virtuous character of any man could interest me, as I am now situated, it is that of Lord Camden; and I hope you will think so when I tell you, that to ease his government I have consented that I should contradict my own order, and I should go into the South to compose the disturbances that now prevail in certain districts in the provinces of Leinster and Munster. Before I yielded these points, I informed my brother officers that I expected soon to be relieved. This I considered as an attention due to myself, and I hope my letter is conceived in such terms as to preclude any misconstruction, or even the most distant idea of my endeavouring to create in the minds of others any improper sentiment or sensation. It must, however, be considered as a pledge that I shall not on any account remain in the chief command in this country. Although I have consented to the revocation of my own order, I cannot consent to my remaining a degraded man. As to the propriety of the order, I trust that I shall hereafter be found to stand on the firmest ground."

The temper and moderation with which Sir Ralph acted on this occasion must be strongly felt, when it is recollected that the proclamation of the 18th May had been practically abandoned in Ireland and disapproved in England, but had not been recalled by proclamation, in order to spare the Government the pain of publicly condemning their own act. Lord Camden, at the instigation of his advisers, condescended to revise and to rest on that order only as the means of placing Sir Ralph in an embarrassing position. Sir Ralph was touched by the pitiable condition of Lord Camden, whose intentions were good, but who was irresolute, and suffered himself to be driven into courses which he did not in his heart approve.

Sir Ralph also clearly saw that some great change in the condition of Ireland must speedily arise, and he was unwilling that his measures, which were intended to arrest, should be falsely represented as being the cause of the impending crisis. While, in compliance with the earnest solicitation of Lord Camden, he recalled the order, he protected himself and prevented any misapprehension as to the real source of the recal, by at the same time announcing to the Army that he was speedily to retire from his command.

The spirit in which Sir Ralph endeavoured to compose the disturbances in the South, is clearly shown in the instructions given to the general officers, in which they are told "that a public notice has been issued by the Commander-in-Chief, calling upon the people to deliver up the arms which have been taken from the Yeomanry and the well-affected; that the general officers are to communicate to the people through the priests, and by one or two men selected from each townland; that if the order is complied with, it will be a sign of their repentance, and that not only forgiveness but protection will follow; that they must be sensible that it is infinitely better for them to remain quietly at home minding their own affairs, than to be committing acts which would ruin them and their families; that as it would be impossible to prevent the innocent from suffering in some degree with the guilty, the innocent have the means of redress by informing against those who have engaged in unlawful associations, and in robbing houses of arms and money.

" The people must be very ignorant not to know, that notwithstanding the fair promises of the French, they have first deceived and then plundered every country into which they have come; and they are forewarned, that in case of invasion, and if they should attempt to join the enemy, or communicate with him, or join in any insurrection, they will be immediately put to death, and their houses and properties destroyed.

"The people ought to know that they cannot expect any redress of matters which they think they have to complain of, while they continue turbulent and giving offence to Government, by joining in acts which disturb the public peace and threaten the lives and properties of loyal subjects.

"The general officers will endeavour to get at the bottom and meaning of the real designs of the instigators of disaffection, to know who they are, and to what length they have proceeded, whether they are banditti taking advantage of the times to rob their neighbours, or whether they proceed from the association called 'United Irishmen,' and are directed by them, or are ebullitions caused by the ferment which has been made, but which has broken out contrary to their present intention.

"In general, to give confidence and courage to the well-affected by promising assistance and protection, and raising the spirits of the magistracy and gentry, pointing out that unless they exert themselves the troops can only be a temporary security to them, and that nothing can really re-establish the government of this country, but enforcing a due execution of the law."

After some observations on the cautious use of secret service-money, and the maintenance of the discipline of the troops, it is added,—"The following questions may be pertinently put. Why should the people be less attached to their Government than they were twelve months ago, when they showed so much loyalty in assisting his Majesty's troops to oppose the French? Is it not because they have been seduced by wicked men? and why should they think themselves bound by oaths into which they have been seduced or terrified?"

Such was the spirit in which Sir Ralph endeavoured to compose the disturbances in the south, which, especially in the county of Tipperary, had assumed a serious character. These disturbances he attributed to the influence of demagogues and of a hostile press acting on the people, who were depressed by the low price of grain, to the severity with which the middlemen exacted their rents, to the abandonment of their duty by the gentry, who quitted their dwellings and retired into towns, and to the violences of religious differences. He particularly called the attention of Government to the fact that in the district to the north of Fethard, the gentry had done their duty, and, with the aid of the Yeomanry, had effectually succeeded in preserving the peace of the country, and on the whole he was of opinion that, by a judicious distribution and employment of the military force, order might speedily be re-established for the time.

That such a spirit was cordially disapproved by the advisers of Lord Camden need hardly be stated, and Sir Ralph's conduct was severely censured by them. Sir Ralph always maintained that military law ought to be confined to those districts which were refractory, and which could not be controlled by the power of the civil authority. All his orders were based on this distinction, and the officers were enjoined to enforce them with the utmost leniency. This was not the opinion of Lord Castlereagh, who had succeeded Mr. Pelham as Chief-Secretary, and to whom Sir Ralph expressed his desire that the proclamation should be enforced in the county of Kilkenny in the most restricted sense, and in the most lenient manner. Lord Castlereagh said that such was not his view, and that coercive measures ought to be left to take their course as the country desired it.

On the 25th April, General Lake was appointed Commander-in-Chief in Ireland, and the consequences of the change are most significantly expressed in the following order, which was issued by General Sir James Stuart at Cork on the 7th of May. "Whereas, it has been reported to General Sir James Stuart, that in some parts of the county where it has been necessary to place troops at free-quarters for the restoration of tranquillity, that general subscriptions have been entered into by the inhabitants to purchase provisions for the troops, by which means the end proposed of making the burthen fall as much as possible on the guilty, is entirely defeated by making it fall in a light proportion on the whole, and thereby easing and protecting the guilty: It has been thought proper to direct that whenever the practice has been adopted or shall be attempted, the general officers commanding divisions in the southern district shall immediately *double, triple, and quadruple the number of soldiers so stationed, and shall send out foraging parties* to provide provisions for the troops in the quantities mentioned in the former notice, bearing date the 27th day of April, and that they shall move them from station to station through the district or barony *until* all *arms* are *surrendered* and *tran-*

quillity be *perfectly restored,* and until it is reported to the *general officers* by the GENTLEMEN HOLDING LANDED PROPERTY, and those who are employed in *collecting* the *public revenue* and *tithes* that ALL RENTS, TAXES, AND TITHES ARE COMPLETELY PAID UP."

A historian of these times has remarked that, after diligent search, he has been unable to find in the proceedings of the French, either under the Republic or under Napoleon, any parallel to the severity and injustice of this order. It can excite no surprise, that the same people who, in the preceding year, had displayed so much loyalty in resisting the French, were, within three weeks from the date of this order, driven into rebellion.

In the month of April, Sir Ralph returned to England, and was instantly appointed to the command of the forces in Scotland. While this appointment was a decided and just tribute to the ability and uprightness of Sir Ralph, and was a proof of the great confidence which the King and his Ministers reposed in him, they did not foresee that when he left Ireland, the last hope of peace was extinguished, and that the burst of military violence which followed his resignation was so soon to involve the country in the horrors of civil war. The remark of Mr. Grattan, "that the policy of Sir Ralph was sound and wise, but that he came a little too late," might have accounted for the failure of that policy, if it had ever been fairly tested. But that remark could not justify the relaxation of discipline, the subversion of the law, and the neglect of the means by which a deluded and oppressed people might have been reclaimed and saved, and still less could it be urged as an apology for the cruelty and tyranny practised by a vindictive Government and a licentious army. The result was, that the English Government decided and acted when it really and certainly was too late. Lord Camden was recalled, and replaced by Lord Cornwallis.

The first act of Lord Cornwallis, on receiving his appointment, was to write to Sir Ralph, and request that he would leave any person who had been on his staff, and in whom he had confidence, who could fully explain the views and policy on which he had acted while he held the command in Ireland. Accordingly, Colonel Hay, who was afterwards killed at the Helder, was left, and remained for some months on the staff of Lord Cornwallis.

When Sir Ralph returned to London, he naturally presented himself on the first occasion at the King's *levée.* The attendance at *levées* was then so limited, that the King walked about, and spoke to those who were present in such order as he chose. Several times the King came very close to Sir Ralph, and always turned aside, so that Sir Ralph began to think that the King did not intend to notice him. At last, however, the King came and addressed these words to him :—" They have used you very ill in Ireland, and you are now going to Scotland, where they will know how to respect you, and to treat you better." When the King retired into his closet, he said to one of his Ministers, " I watched my opportunity, when certain Irish politicians were within hearing, and I took good care that they should be in no doubt as to my opinion of Sir Ralph and his conduct."

The following letters from Sir Ralph may properly be annexed to this brief account of his conduct in Ireland, as they illustrate the view which he took of his own position, and of the future prospects of a country in whose welfare he was so warmly interested. The two first letters are addressed to his eldest son, and the third to a military friend.

On the 1st April 1798, Sir Ralph thus writes from Dublin :—" In a letter to my brother, I informed him that I had desired to be recalled from my present command. This step is no doubt unfortunate at this moment, but it is much better for the King's service and for Lord Camden's Government that a successor should be sent over, than that there should exist an open war between my Lord-Lieutenant's cabinet and myself. The breach is too wide to be closed, and they and I must be always at variance. They will never forgive me, because they know that they have not only injured me, but have used every means in their power to ruin me, and it is impossible that I can ever have any confidence in men who have endeavoured to deprive me of my good name. I shall not enter at present into any detail on my own conduct since I came to Ireland. I trust that it is irreproachable, and that I have reason on my side. It is some satisfaction to have the opinion of the reasonable men, both civil and military, with me, and that the man,[1] not the last in this kingdom, is among the number.

"The hue and cry has been raised in London by letters from hence, and has been carried on, as I hear, principally by that immaculate character, Lord Auckland. I shall keep my temper, and patiently wait for the moment when I can be heard. My Lord Camden has begged of me to go to the South,

[1] Lord Camden.

to endeavour to compose the disturbances that prevail in that part of the country. I could not refuse his Lordship, although I know the drift of it, and that he has been advised to put this service on me.

"This is a most wretched country. The upper orders have fallen into a lethargy, and are only occupied in eating and drinking, or in uttering their unmanly fears. They know that they have been the oppressors of the poor, and that the moment of vengeance is at hand. The lower orders rejoice that in their opinion the moment is at hand when they can glut their revenge, and hope for a more equal share of the good things in this life."

On the 20th April 1798, Sir Ralph writes from Dublin :—" I returned last night from the South. I had reason, from the proclamation and instructions I received, to believe that an insurrection had taken place in the province of Munster. I have been through all the disaffected districts, and found nothing but tranquillity, the people employed in cultivating their lands and following their usual avocations. They were civil and submissive, and although I never took any escort or anything more than one servant, I was under no apprehension, even the most distant, of any danger. Several robberies have been committed, as has been at all times the custom in this country; some private quarrels have been avenged, and arms have been taken from the Protestants. The people, however, are induced to give them up, partly through fear, partly through persuasion. I do not, however, doubt, that if an enemy should land, the Roman Catholics will rise and cut the throats of the Protestants.

"I really think Lord Camden is ill-advised to declare the kingdom in rebellion, and to establish something more than martial law over the whole kingdom. It was perhaps right to do something in that way in some particular districts where the greatest outrages had been committed, and where the magistrates had fled from their duty. I am now convinced that a writ may be executed in any part of Ireland. Do not, therefore, be under any immediate apprehension about this country. My resignation being accepted, and having refused any compromise, which could not have produced any confidence, I shall leave this country as soon as General Lake relieves me. I once more beg all my friends will be easy on my account."

The following letter expresses the opinion of Sir Ralph at so late a period as the 28th January 1799.

"I am not afraid of being charged with prejudices.

If I have any, they are in favour of a country in which I have lived long, in which I formed many valuable friendships, some of which are still fresh in my mind. There cannot be a subject more interesting than that of your letter. Long observation has convinced me, that all your misfortunes, that all the evils with which you are threatened, proceed from the illiberal, the unjust, and the unwise conduct of England. Your Legislature and your Executive Government partake of course, of the vices flowing from the wretched system of English domination. The vices of the Government infect the manners of the people. If I find a peasantry cunning, deceitful, lazy, and vindictive, I cannot attribute it, without impiety, to the hand of God. It must come from the iron hand of man. Although the French Revolution and Jacobin principles may be the immediate cause of the events which have lately taken place in Ireland, yet the remote and ultimate cause must be derived from its true origin, the oppression of centuries. Do not imagine that I am weak enough to believe that a few effusions of lenity or benevolence are to soften or subdue the minds of a people hardened by oppression. It will require the wisest system you can devise, and length of time, to effect it. In the meantime, you must trust to the due execution of the Law, and to a powerful and well disciplined Army for your protection. The Irish people are not a thinking people, they have strong prejudices. However, people will think for them. Till a new system has begun to take effect, they will remain the tools of a foreign enemy, or of domestic agitators and demagogues. God grant that the measures on the affairs of Ireland, which, they say, are now under consideration, may be well weighed, and that the spirit of party may give way to true wisdom."

Sir Ralph's own letters explain his conduct and unfold his views with so much clearness and simplicity, that it is unnecessary, and perhaps scarcely justifiable, to make any addition to them. Sir Ralph held the chief command in Ireland from the beginning of December 1797, to the month of April following. The times were difficult and critical, especially for the officer to whom the command of the Army was intrusted. The objects to which his attention was necessarily directed, were the restoration of the discipline of the Army, so that it might be in a condition to contend with the enemy in the event of an invasion by the French, the maintenance of public tranquillity, and the efficient protection of life and property. The peculiarity of the case was that the first and indispensable means to be taken for the restoration of discipline, was to abandon the vicious practice of scattering the troops in small parties over the whole face of the country, for the protection of those who were unwilling to make any effort for their own security. The Commander-in-Chief was forced to call the immediate attention of the Lord-Lieutenant, and of his Government, to the necessity of drawing the troops together in larger numbers, in order that discipline might be restored and enforced, and he advised that the preservation of domestic tranquillity should be left to the large body of Yeomanry, which had been raised for that especial purpose, and that the aid of the Army should only be required in urgent cases, and on the demand of the civil power.

It is obvious that in such a state of affairs, the civil and military policy of the country were so intimately blended, that separation was impossible. It is also obvious that the discussion of such questions could not be conducted without more or less involving the fundamental policy of the Government. Sir Ralph was responsible for the discipline of an Army which might at any moment be called upon to act against the enemy, and he would have ill discharged his duty to his country, if he had tamely acquiesced in a system which was destructive of all hope of improvement, and had relied for the defence of his inaction, on the ground that it was not his duty, as a soldier, to interfere with the domestic policy of the Government, who were entitled to require the service of the Army in whatever way appeared to them to be most expedient for the public advantage.

No man, as has been shown, was more earnestly desirous to restore and maintain the proper and constitutional relations between the civil and military power than Sir Ralph, and his interference with the civil policy of the country was forced upon him by an imperative sense of duty, and by the danger to the public safety in the event of the expected invasion being realized. That Sir Ralph conducted his communications with the Lord-Lieutenant on these delicate and important questions, with temper, firmness, and good sense, is clearly established by the letters of Lord Camden to the Duke of Portland. It is fortunate for the fame of Sir Ralph, that in the midst of such difficulties, he was enabled, even during the short period of his command, to develop his humanity, his love of justice, and his respect for the law; to display the sagacity of a wise statesman in discerning the policy that was best calculated to extricate Ireland from the serious and urgent difficulties in which it was involved. Having matured his opinion he took his part with decision, and maintained it with unflinching consistency and resolution. As Commander of the Forces, he struggled to protect the people by restraining the licentiousness of the troops, he made the most strenuous efforts to restore the discipline and efficiency of the Army, and to re-establish those relations between the civil and military power which are prescribed by the Law and the Constitution. The military Commander had to contend with the inveterate vices of the system that prevailed, with the infirm and irresolute mind of the Lord-Lieutenant, and with the unscrupulous and vindictive characters of his advisers; and having no support but that which he might conciliate by the justice and wisdom of his measures, it is plain that nothing but the most entire devotion to his duty, and to the interests of his country, would have induced one so calm and circumspect as Sir Ralph, to engage in a contest with such a host of formidable opponents. He courted no party, he sought no allies; he was facile on small, and uncompromising on great points; he stood alone, trusting to the justice of his Sovereign, and to the dispassionate judgment of his country. His reliance was not misplaced; for although the influence of a most powerful Irish party, acting on the ignorance of the English public, succeeded in raising a fearful storm against him, he remained unmoved, and did not seek the honour of martyrdom, but waited patiently for the development of those events which he felt convinced would justify the course he had taken, and he was sustained by receiving the prompt and cordial approval of his Sovereign.

On resigning the command in Ireland, Sir Ralph was appointed Commander of the Forces in Scotland, and in a letter dated the 14th May 1798, he thus expresses himself:—"It seems determined that I must accept of the command in Scotland; it is by no means with my good-will, as it will expose me to more company and expense than I could wish, and can add neither to my fortune nor my fame. Were I to choose, I should have said, allow me to be quiet till there is occasion for me. But the King is determined to give me the highest mark in his power, on account of the injury done to the service, not in removing me, but in removing his Commander-in-Chief by a political blast."

While Sir Ralph was residing in Scotland, as Commander of the Forces, he received a letter from his valued and attached friend, General (afterwards Lord) Hutchinson, who was then at Dundalk. The letter was dated from Dundalk on the 12th June 1799, and as it not only contains the opinions of the General with respect to the state of Ireland, but refers also to the expediency of making a diversion in favour of the Allies by a descent on Holland, it forms an appropriate conclusion to the account of Sir Ralph's service in Ireland, and an introduction to the Dutch expedition, which is the next important event in the career of Sir Ralph, and therefore it is here inserted. "I was sent down here to command a brigade of English militia a few days after the French left Brest. Two of my regiments have returned to England. One of them, the Warwick, would stay no longer. The King of England has a great number of armed men in his service, but where his army is, I am at a great loss to find.

"In my opinion, the Rebellion in this country is entirely put down. The rebels seem to be sick of their own machinations, by which they have been themselves the chief sufferers. I suppose you know that I support the Union. After all my patriotism, I have been obliged to vote for the annihilation of the Irish Legislature, but such are the hopes of man, and such the termination of his most proud designs. And yet I never was so convinced of anything in politics, as of the necessity of this measure. If ever there was a country unfit to govern itself, it is Ireland : a corrupt aristocracy, a ferocious commonalty, a distracted government, a divided people. I solemnly believe that the great mass of every religious persuasion in this country have no wish so near their hearts, as to enjoy the power of persecuting each other. The Catholic would murder the Protestant in the name of God ; the Protestant would murder the Catholic in the name of law. Both sects seem to consider their common country only as an extended field of battle, where each are at full liberty to display their sanguinary dexterity. The bulk of the people, in my opinion, are by no means averse to the Union. The south is certainly for it ; the north silent ; Dublin clamorous ; the lawyers outrageous ; the chief opposition will, therefore, be in Parliament, where money and influence can do everything. But Lord Castlereagh will be deceived, if he thinks that he can pay the needy members of Parliament in sentences and not in cash. The fact is, people are so used to be bribed in this country, that they will not even do what is right, or their own business, unless they are paid for it.

"The success of the Allies on the Continent has been greater than could have been reasonably expected. The Archduke will soon again act offensively on the Upper Rhine. The French cannot be enabled to leave many troops in Holland. Now would be the moment (and moments are everything in war), to make a diversion, and put the project of the summer of 1795 in execution. Certainly it ought to be easy now to assemble from fifteen to twenty thousand men. It would surely not be difficult to get volunteers from the militia, both English and Irish." After enlarging on the advantages which might result from such an employment of the military force of England, and expressing his apprehensions as to the course likely to be pursued by the King of Prussia, who, he thinks, must see the aggrandizement of Austria and the destruction of French power with an evil eye, as it was only the predominant genius of Frederick that ever could have made the house of Brandenburgh a match for the House of Austria, he thus concludes, "Since I have written what precedes, I find from Mr. Dundas' motion in the House of Commons for an act of Parliament to allow twenty thousand of the militia to enlist in the regular forces, that some project of an extended kind is in contemplation. In that event, if they are wise, they will give you the command. You have local knowledge, and experience of the modern manner of warfare, which the grandees of our army want. I need not again repeat to you that I shall be ready to attend you in any capacity, even that of a friend. My passion for fighting rather increases than diminishes; besides, I have a great idea that the French are just as easily beaten as other people. I think in our time we did not find them much greater heroes than ourselves. We lost more ground by our own weakness than by their prowess."

CHAPTER V.

EXPEDITION TO HOLLAND.

1799.

THE success of the allied armies against the French in Southern Germany and in Northern Italy in the year 1799, together with the willingness of the Emperor Paul to send his Russians to act against the French wherever their services were to be paid for, suggested to the English Ministers the expediency of making a diversion in favour of the Allies, and of attempting to restore the independence of Holland.

As a preliminary step for this object a treaty was concluded in the month of June 1799 between the English Government and the Emperor of Russia, by which these powers became bound to furnish a force to the amount, and on the conditions therein specified. It was stipulated that the united force should be placed under the command of the Duke of York, and should, in the first instance, be employed in expelling the French from the United

Provinces, and that, if successful, their operations should not be confined to Holland.

If a really powerful diversion could have been made by England and Russia in Holland at a proper moment, it might have been attended with very beneficial results to the cause of the Allies. The expulsion of the French, and the restoration of the Prince of Orange as Stadtholder, and the re-establishment of the independence of Holland—in whose fate, as well as that of the Low Countries, England had the deepest interest—were objects, if attainable, of sufficient importance to have amply justified the prudence of the treaty concluded with Russia. In addition to these considerations, a very strong belief prevailed that the Dutch were so discontented and so hostile to the French that they would instantly rally round the standard of the Prince of Orange, as soon as it was raised with any prospect of support and success.

Such being the views of the projectors of the expedition, it is obvious that obtaining possession of the Dutch fleet, on which so much stress was ultimately laid, entered very little, if at all, into the contemplation of the projectors of the expedition. When, in addition to the considerations already stated, the serious consequences which must result from the great struggle in which Europe was then, and for so many succeeding years, involved, were deliberately weighed, it is not surprising that the English Ministers were tempted by the prosperous efforts of the Allies, to make as powerful a diversion as they could in their favour in the hope of terminating a war in which the treasure and blood of England were so freely lavished.

Even now, when the wisdom of having engaged in the expedition to Holland has been tested by the event, it must be admitted that the opportunity was most inviting, for we were committed in a great contest, and the professed objects, if attained, would have been an ample compensation for the expense to be incurred and the risk to be run; but it was a fatal fault that the Ministers were too sanguine, and were misled by their zeal in the cause; they resolved to act and were pledged to the enterprise before they had obeyed the dictates of prudence, by maturely weighing the difficulties that were to be overcome, and carefully considering how their means could be most usefully employed, and how far they were sufficient for the attainment of the objects which they had in view.

The most superficial glance at the perils which are inseparable from maritime expeditions must increase regret that the fame of the English Army and the honour of the country were hastily committed to so hazardous an enterprise.

The assembling of men, ships of war, and transports, the time necessary for the embarkation of infantry, cavalry, artillery, ammunition and stores, can scarcely fail to enable the enemy to penetrate the objects of such preparations and to take the necessary measures to resist and defeat them. The wind and weather exercise a great and controlling influence on the movements of a fleet, with respect to the moment of departure, during the voyage, at the time of landing on the coast of the enemy, and in supplying the troops with all necessary requisites, until they have gained as much ground in the country invaded as will enable them to maintain themselves. Such dangers are beyond control, and no human skill or foresight can avert them. It will be seen that the expedition to Holland did not escape these perils, which had not been overlooked by Sir Ralph when he was required to pronounce an opinion on the prudence of the enterprise, and on the plans that were submitted to him. The unfavourable state of the wind and weather after the fleet left the English shore, fully justified the wisdom of duly calculating on such incidents, and caused delays which very materially increased the difficulties and the hazard of the enterprise. The Russian troops also in their voyage from the North were exposed to similar perils from adverse wind and weather.

Having concluded the Treaty with Russia, the Ministers then began to collect and form the English army, and vessels for their transport, and to deliberate on and decide the plan of operations.

While these proceedings were in progress, Sir Ralph was employed in the command of the forces in Scotland, and it was not until after the Treaty with Russia had been concluded, and progress had been made in collecting the troops, that he was summoned to London, and made acquainted with the views and intentions of the Ministers. As Sir Ralph was subsequently intrusted with the command of the first division of the English army, and took so very prominent a part throughout the expedition, it is desirable to trace, with as much accuracy as is now practicable, the extent of the responsibility which he incurred, and the opinions which he formed and submitted to the Ministers on the expediency and wisdom of this great enterprise.

The first communication made to Sir Ralph was

in a letter received by him in Edinburgh, from Mr. Dundas, dated on the 8th June 1799.[1]

Mr. Dundas, in the letter to which reference has been made, stated "That although there is never dependence to be placed on the disposition of Prussia, governed as she is, by a corrupted and weak administration, still she must be ready, if actuated either by her fears or her interest she shall be induced to come forward. By our most recent intelligence it is not impossible that at any hour she may call upon France to evacuate Holland, with a menace of marching a Prussian army into it, if she does not. If she takes this step, she will at the same time call upon us to co-operate with our fleet, and to seize on the island of Walcheren. We must be ready if such an event takes place, and I have this morning arranged with the Duke of York to carry the accompanying disposition of troops into execution. I have not time to enter into farther

---

[1] It may not be without interest to mention a characteristic incident which has been preserved by a friend who had been much associated with Sir Ralph in early life. "I breakfasted," says this friend, "with Sir Ralph the day before he left Edinburgh to take the command of the expedition to Holland in 1799. I found him in great spirits, and, what I less expected, Lady Abercromby was perfectly calm and tranquil. On remarking this to Sir Ralph, he replied, I have an excellent wife, who, without a murmur, allows me to go where I please." This incident marks the promptitude with which Sir Ralph sacrificed the ease of domestic life to every opportunity of serving his country. It shows how completely a knowledge of the ruling passion of her husband had taught a devoted wife to control and keep in subjection her warmest affections, under most trying circumstances.

details, but if you wish to command the expedition, you must come away as soon as you can after the receipt of this letter." On the same day that Sir Ralph received this letter from Mr. Dundas, he also received a letter from Colonel Brownrigg, written by command of the Duke of York, asking what general officers and staff he would wish to accompany him on the expedition which it was proposed to place under his command. It will be observed that the expedition of which Sir Ralph is invited by Mr. Dundas to take the command, is far different from that which was eventually carried into execution. An attack on the island of Walcheren, with a view of assisting the expected invasion of Holland by a Prussian army, is the object proposed to Sir Ralph. There is no mention of the treaty with Russia which was then on the eve of being signed, and there is no allusion to an invasion of Holland by an allied force under the command of the Duke of York.

At what precise time the hopes of an invasion of Holland by the Prussians were abandoned does not appear, but they seem to have been cherished so late as the 20th of July, when Sir Ralph was instructed to prepare a short statement of the effect that might be anticipated from an attack by the

Meuse on the province of Holland, and of the facilities that it would give to an enemy intending to act in the direction in which it was supposed that the Prussians would move. The statement was intended to enable Mr. Grenville, then at Berlin, to show that the plan of attacking Holland by the Meuse would render the movement of the Prussians safe and easy; but the opinion of Mr. Dundas that no reliance could be placed on the steadiness of Prussian policy, seems to have been completely verified. Early in August the English Government were in possession of the fact that the French Directory had intimated to the King of Prussia that they were prepared to sacrifice the Batavian Republic, and to co-operate with him in restoring the Stadtholder, on the condition of his remaining neuter. On the 7th of August, Lord Grenville wrote to Mr. Dundas, suggesting that Sir Ralph should send an officer with a flag of truce, in the first instance to the Governor of the Brille, with a summons for the surrender of that place, but charged with a demand for a passport to the Hague, to carry there a proposal for the peaceful re-establishment of the ancient government; and the officer might be directed to declare in conversation to all whom he should see, that the French

Directory had offered to sacrifice the Batavian Republic and to restore the Stadtholder, provided they would remain neuter. The suggestion of Lord Grenville proceeds on the assumption that the proposal of the French Directory would be rejected by the King of Prussia. It occurred, on the other hand, to Sir Ralph that it was possible that the proposal might be accepted, and he asked how he was to conduct himself if, in consequence of a treaty between France and Prussia, any of the troops of the latter power should have entered Holland. The only reply was, that in such event he must act according to circumstances, and to the dictates of his own discretion. Sir Ralph, seeing the doubt and irresolution of the Ministers with regard to the issue of the proposal made by France to Prussia, was much embarrassed and dissatisfied with the vagueness of a reply, which, instead of giving him instructions for the regulation of his conduct, was calculated to throw upon him a responsibility properly belonging to the advisers of the Crown.

When the hopes of an invasion of Holland by the Prussians died away, then the necessity for finding employment for the English and Russian force, according to the terms of the Treaty, became pressing and urgent. The invasion of Holland was the professed object, but how, or in what direction it should be attempted, was a question towards the solution of which no real progress had been made.

On Sir Ralph arriving in London, he was placed in command of the forces that were assembling on the coast of Kent, and Mr. Pitt and Mr. Dundas took up their residence at Walmer Castle, that they might have frequent and easy communication with him, as soon as the expected reports of Johnstone, a well-known smuggler, who was employed by the Government to collect information as to what was passing on the coast of Holland, had been received. Many plans were proposed, much discussion ensued, and in fact no positive and final decision had been reached when the expedition was on the eve of sailing. It will appear from the letters which will be hereafter inserted, that Sir Ralph from the first was strongly impressed with the difficulties that were to be encountered, and he was of opinion that the risk which must be run, and the perils to which the Army must be exposed were so great, that they could not be justified by the importance of the objects to which our efforts were to be directed. He stated his views to the Ministers most frankly and unreservedly, so much so, indeed, that Mr. Pitt, who was unacquainted with the details of military operations, and with the means that were required to afford a reasonable chance of success, could not always repress his impatience, and on one occasion remarked, very pointedly, "There are some persons who have a pleasure in opposing whatever is proposed." Sir Ralph was not moved by this hint, and he persevered in expressing his opinions with calmness and firmness.

It would now be superfluous to discuss the merits of the many projects that were suggested and considered, as the opinion of Sir Ralph was alike unfavourable to all, and his responsibility was ultimately limited to the adoption of the plan for landing at the Helder, with a view to the capture of the Dutch fleet, which he throughout regarded as the most promising object that had been proposed. The views of the Ministers, and the grounds on which the country was committed to this great enterprise, cannot be more accurately represented than by a faithful abstract of the instructions given to Sir Ralph previously to the sailing of the first division of the English Army, which took place on the 13th of August.

The first instruction is dated on the 3d of August,

and states that the object of the treaty with the Emperor of Russia was to rescue Holland from the tyranny of the French, and to restore its independence; that the forces to be employed on this service were to proceed in different divisions, and that the first division was placed under the command of Sir Ralph, and was directed to proceed to the entrance of the Meuse, and to obtain possession of Goree, Over Flacken, the small island of Romburg, and that of Voorne. It assumed that the three first islands might easily be taken, but Voorne, possessing two towns regularly fortified, might require more serious military operations; and it specified that a most confident expectation was entertained that these islands might be secured. The object of the campaign, after the arrival of reinforcements, was, the instruction continued, if possible to obtain possession of the provinces north of the Waal before the bad weather set in, and therefore it became desirable to seize upon some point on the mainland where the troops could be at once disembarked as they successively arrived. The selection of the position on the mainland was left to the discretion of the commander, but Maasland, Sluys, Schiedam, Rotterdam, and Dort, are designated as the points most desirable with reference to the object in view.

This instruction indicates clearly that the first plan was to attack Voorne, to gain, if possible, a footing on the mainland; and that the ultimate object of the campaign was to obtain possession of the Provinces of the Union, north of the Waal.

In a second instruction, dated on the 4th of August, and supplementary to that of the 3d of August, Mr. Dundas states that he feels it to be due to the public service and to Sir Ralph to state the grounds on which the instructions had been framed, and the peculiar motives which had led to the decision that the expedition should proceed without delay to the place of destination. Mr. Dundas admits that the returns and reports which he had received from Sir Ralph, since he took the command at Barham camp, had made such an impression on his mind as might have induced him humbly to advise his Majesty to suspend any attempt against Holland until the first division of the Russian army should arrive at Yarmouth, or a considerable addition could be made to the British troops by the reinforcements now collecting from the militia of the kingdom. Mr. Dundas proceeds to remark, that had he felt it to have been his duty to submit that advice to his Majesty, it would not have been founded so much upon any apprehension that with the present numbers the danger of the enterprise would be of such a magnitude that in prudence it ought not to be undertaken, or that the object was not of sufficient importance to warrant that reasonable degree of risk to which every great military operation is liable, as upon the opinion he had formed that the present force, should it have been found adequate to the reduction of the islands in the mouth of the Meuse, would not, however, have been able to follow up that success immediately, and to improve it by such further operations, as in every military view of the question it would be highly desirable that Sir Ralph should have the means of proceeding upon without any interruption or delay, of which the enemy, if not prevented by the want of resources, or the favourable disposition of the country, might have availed themselves to throw many obstacles in the way of future operations. Mr. Dundas, in the same instruction, goes on to observe, that having thought it right so far to state the leading motives which would have induced him to concur in recommending that the departure of the expedition should be deferred until it could be reinforced, had he been called upon to decide on military considerations only; he adds, that he would have been the more inclined to admit of delay, from a wish to remove entirely the chance of a failure at the outset, which, however improbable with the present force, had not been perhaps so completely guarded against as might have been the case, had he been at liberty to waive other essential considerations consequent upon a full review of the political relations of Great Britain with other powers as connected with this expedition, the general state of Europe, and other motives arising out of internal arrangements too urgent to allow of the expedition being retarded until it could be further reinforced.

Mr. Dundas, in the same communication, states the great importance he attaches to Sir Ralph being in a position to follow up his first operations with as little delay as possible, and he assures him that he has felt it to be his duty to require from every department of Government the utmost exertions for bringing forward every further means the country could afford, to be ready to support Sir Ralph within the least possible time after his departure. The instruction concludes with details relative to the amount of reinforcements proposed to be sent, and with the expression of a confident hope that no disappointment would arise on that point. The whole spirit of this instruction is a frank and candid recognition of the weight which was felt to be due to objections that had been pressed by Sir Ralph, and Mr. Dundas, with his characteristic boldness, at once assumes the whole responsibility as resting on himself and his colleagues.

There is a third instruction, dated on the 5th of August, of which the object is to point out the political conduct to be observed when the troops shall have made good their landing in the United Provinces. A proclamation, setting forth that the object of the Allies was the expulsion of the French, the restoration of the independence of Holland, and of the former Government, under the chief direction of the Stadtholder, and an address from the Prince of Orange was also to be disseminated as widely as possible. The only paragraph in the proclamation to which it is requisite to make special reference, is that in which it is stated that it is "not his Majesty's intention by the proclamation, or by any other declaration to be made in his Majesty's name, to preclude himself from supporting, or even recommending, such alterations in the Dutch constitution, as, being conformable to the ancient principles of that Government, may be necessary for giving it more vigour and energy." No opportunity was ever offered for testing the object or spirit in which this part of the instruction was framed.

The preceding instructions were followed by another, which is dated on the 10th of August. This latter instruction, it is stated, is founded on intelligence collected respecting the approach to Helvoetsluys, and that on a comparison of the objections arising out of that intelligence with the plan pointed out in the instruction No. 1, the conduct of the commander is to be governed by the following considerations, namely,—that according to advices recently received from the Continent, the immediate sailing of the expedition is a matter of most urgent necessity, and that, as there appears to be very little doubt of being able to take possession of Goree, it is in any case to be considered as the first object. Goree being secured, it is then left to the judgment of the General and Admiral to determine whether the facility it will afford is sufficient to warrant the attempt against Voorne. In the event of the decision being that the attack on Voorne is impracticable, or that the hazard is greater than it would be reasonable to incur, then the next object of immediate importance is to attempt to get possession of the Helder and the Texel Island, with the probability of obtaining the disposal of the Dutch navy. The mode of making the attack, as well as the expediency of its being undertaken, is left to the discretion of Sir Ralph, after receiving the report of the officer who had been sent to Lord Duncan to obtain information, and such suggestions as he might offer. Should the attack both on Voorne and the Helder be relinquished, it is stated that there appears to be little doubt of the facility with which troops might enter the Ems, to be landed in the neighbourhood of Delfzyl, and thence to push their operations in such a manner as might be best adapted to reduce the provinces of Groningen and Friesland, and the generality of Drenthe. The instruction adds, " details have been avoided, wishing to leave entirely to the judgment of Sir Ralph the direction of the movements of his army according to the intelligence he may procure on the spot, of the strength of the enemy, the disposition of the inhabitants, and other circumstances, which must direct him in the execution of a plan of this nature. Should he," the instruction continues, " be compelled to make the conquest of Groningen the principal object of his attack, provision shall be made for supplying him immediately with a reinforcement of cavalry." Sir Ralph was not restricted from proceeding with his whole force to the Helder, if that should be the selected point of attack, but it was recommended that, if practicable, he should send a detachment to Goree, sufficient to hold it for a few days, until it could be reinforced from England, on the ground that the friends of the Prince of Orange might have made their arrangements in the belief that that island would be at once occupied by an English force. The instruction concludes by stating that the exercise of Sir Ralph's own discretion, in concert with the Admiral, is not excluded from modifying each or either of these plans, or from adopting any other, the Government being satisfied that their efforts will be directed to whatever object may appear most to correspond with the advantage of the King's service, and the spirit of the instructions.

These instructions show that the Ministers had matured no plan on which they could confidently rely, and by which they were prepared to abide; but the attack on the islands of Goree and of Voorne had been so definitively fixed, that it had been announced to those in Holland with whom they had been in correspondence, and they, it was reasonable to conclude, must have made their arrangements under the belief that these islands, or Goree at least, would be occupied by an English force. The Ministers must, therefore, naturally have been reluctant to abandon that portion of a plan to which they were committed, and thus to disappoint the hopes and defeat the arrangements of their friends, and to betray a vacillation which could not fail to abate the confidence of those who might be disposed to co-operate with the English in restoring the independence of their country.

Recent information as to the difficulty of approach to Helvoetsluys, is assigned as the reason for this change of plan, and yet it could scarcely be the real one, as it was a port that had been so constantly and so frequently resorted to by English vessels, that accurate information as to the approach to the town must have been easily obtained. Be that as it may, the attack on the Helder is for the first time brought prominently forward in the instruction of the 10th of August, and, failing that, it is suggested, that a landing might be made in the mouth of the Ems, with a view of conquering the provinces of Groningen and Friesland. But so much uncertainty seems to have been felt as to the practicability of executing any of these projects, that Sir Ralph, in conjunction with the Admiral, was authorized " to modify each or either of these plans, or to adopt any other which in their judgment should correspond with the advantage of the King's service, and the spirit of their instructions." The only point on which the instructions were uniform and imperative was, that something must be done, and that the departure of the first division of the Army must be immediate. The necessity which prompted this imperative instruction, was the obligation which England had contracted with her Allies. It was that obligation which decided Mr. Dundas to insist on the departure of the expedition, while he felt and acknowledged the force of the objections which had been urged by Sir Ralph, and which finally sent the first division of the Army to sea without any definite object or plan having been adopted.

The wish to make a powerful diversion in favour of our Allies, to expel the French, and to restore the independence of Holland, were in themselves most laudable and honourable objects, but it must be deeply lamented that a heavy expenditure, and the unfortunate conclusion of a great enterprise, were the results of an engagement which had been entered into without a due appreciation of all the difficulties to be encountered, and without mature consideration how far the means were sufficient to secure the attainment of the proposed ends. These misfortunes might probably have been avoided, if reference had been timeously made to the advice of military men of experience and ability, for it does not appear that, with the exception of unfavourable weather, of which the most was made, any difficulties occurred which could not have been foreseen by commanders of capacity and real knowledge of what was necessary to warrant a probability of ultimate success.

How far the great change of plan between the 3d and 10th of August may have been influenced by the representations of Sir Ralph, cannot now be ascertained by direct evidence. There is, however, abundant proof that throughout he was unfavourable to the enterprise, and that among the different projects which were entertained, he always preferred the attack on the Helder and the capture of the Dutch fleet, as being the most practicable, and the most likely, if successful, to sustain the spirit of the English people in a struggle from which there was no present prospect of escape. No correct judgment can be formed of the opinions which were entertained and expressed by Sir Ralph on this occasion, without adverting to the view which he took of the character and spirit of the War in which the country was embarked. He adhered to the opinion which he had formed at the conclusion of the campaign of 1793, that a great revolution had begun which would not stop until it had shaken and changed the condition of all the nations of Europe. He saw that it was, in spirit, a war against opinion; and recognising the principle that it could not be put down by force, he anxiously longed for the opportunity of retiring from the struggle by making as reasonable and honourable a peace as could be secured. If peace could not be obtained, he was deeply impressed with the importance of preventing the spirit of the country from being broken by repeated defeats which might lead them to make dangerous and dishonourable concessions.

When he was required to form a judgment as to the practicability and wisdom of the enterprise in which he was about to take a part, his views were governed by the opinions which he had so firmly and steadily maintained, and so often expressed. The two points which engaged his attention were the importance of avoiding a disheartening defeat, and of endeavouring so to direct our efforts as to achieve a success that would sustain and animate the spirit of the country. Accordingly, it will be seen that he was never shaken in his opinion that the projected invasion of Holland was an effort beyond our strength and our means, and most likely to end in disappointment or disaster, and that of all the plans suggested the attack on the Helder and the capture of the Dutch fleet was the only one that he was disposed to countenance, as being calculated to support the spirit of the country. Major Kempt, afterwards General Sir James Kempt, who subsequently was appointed to be the Secretary to Sir Ralph, was at that time his first aide-de-camp. The private correspondence did not pass through his hands, but with such great access to know the opinions of Sir Ralph, he entirely confirms the statement now made. When the expedition was on the eve of sailing, Major Kempt was sent by Sir Ralph with a despatch to Mr. Dundas at Sir C. Middleton's, where the Ministers were assembled to attend the King on the occasion of his inspecting the volunteers of the county of Kent, and was directed to return with the utmost speed. The despatch contained a short letter from Sir Ralph to Mr. Dundas, stating that he enclosed a paper which had been drawn up by Sir John Hope under his direction. Mr. Pitt read the paper in the presence of Major Kempt, and he repeatedly expressed his approval of it in the warmest terms. The troops began to embark immediately on the return of Major Kempt. On the evening of the day on which the troops were put on board, Major

Kempt was sent to Ramsgate, to bring General Coote to head-quarters at Deal, to receive further instructions. General Coote's brigade was actually embarked, and he said that he had received his instructions, but they were partially countermanded, and he was directed to make a demonstration on the coast of Holland, remote from the Helder, to distract the attention of the enemy, and he was afterwards to join the main body of the forces.

The order given to General Coote leaves no doubt that Sir Ralph had resolved to exercise the discretion intrusted to him by the instruction of the 10th of August, by directing the attack against the Helder, unless subsequent information should be received from the officer who had been sent to Lord Duncan, and whom he was to meet at sea, or unless he should find that the Admiral entertained a different opinion. Neither of these events, as will appear, happened. The expedition sailed on the 13th of August, and on the 14th, Sir Ralph communicated to Mr. Dundas, that the intelligence brought by the officer who had been sent to Lord Duncan to bring the latest tidings from the coast of Holland, had not shaken his purpose, and that he intended to proceed to the Helder. Admiral Mitchell and Mr. Dundas both expressed their cordial approval of this decision. There are letters written by Sir Ralph to his family during, and after the conclusion of the expedition, in which he expresses his opinion as to the impolicy of the enterprise. It is sufficient for the present purpose to refer to one letter which is addressed to Mr. Huskisson, the Under Secretary of State, who was most intimately acquainted with all the facts, as he enjoyed the unreserved confidence both of Mr. Dundas and of Sir Ralph. In a letter dated on the 10th of October, which will be hereafter more fully noticed, Sir Ralph says, "I am unwilling to write to Mr. Dundas on the subject. My mind always went in opposition to this undertaking, and I spoke my sentiments on it so fully before I left England, that it is decent to be silent in my correspondence with him, on the consequences likely to result from it." It was due to truth and to the judgment to be formed of the military reputation of Sir Ralph to disclose his real opinions, and to show that in his intercourse with the Ministers he had avowed, and expressed his views of the expedition with the frankness and decision which became an independent man, and which was so consistent with his conduct on all occasions.

There has been no desire to cast blame on the

authors of the expedition, for justice and candour exact the unqualified admission, that the importance of the objects they had in view, the urgent pressure of their Allies, and the peculiar character of the contest in which the country was involved, were motives calculated to exercise a most powerful influence over the decisions of capable and honest statesmen. The fault was, that they were too sanguine, that they were not sufficiently impressed or acquainted with the difficulties with which they would have to contend, and that they did not avail themselves of the advice of capable and experienced military men before they were committed to this hazardous undertaking. The opinions of the Ministers and of Sir Ralph, were no doubt materially, and perhaps unconsciously, influenced by the different points of view from which they looked on the spirit of the contest and on the events that were passing. The Ministers were conducting the War under the impression that they could confine France within her former limits, put down the revolutionary spirit and reckless ambition of the French people, and restore the ancient sway of the Bourbons. Sir Ralph did not participate in these sanguine views. He entertained faint hopes of effecting these objects, he was opposed to wasting our resources and risking the fame of the English Army on unprofitable and impracticable objects, and, above all, he feared a repetition of defeat, which he thought would either prolong the War, or lead to an unsatisfactory and insecure peace. Such, no doubt, were the grounds of difference in the views of Sir Ralph, and of those Ministers who had imbibed the spirit of Mr. Burke.

It would be unjust to the memory of Mr. Dundas, who took so prominent a part in the conduct of the War, to withhold the impression that has been made by a careful perusal of his correspondence with Sir Ralph. It is plain that throughout his views were of a more sober and practical nature than those of his more sanguine colleagues. It has been shown how correctly he appreciated the weakness and bad faith of the Prussian Government; and it will appear that he subsequently expressed at least an equal distrust of the policy and power of Austria. The project of a treaty with Russia was conceived and executed under the excitement awakened by the temporary success of the Allies on the Continent. The Emperor of Russia appeared to be, for the time, a sincere ally, and other concomitant circumstances being favourable, Mr. Dundas was induced to concur with his colleagues in concluding the treaty with Russia. Being so committed, with his characteristic manliness he boldly and steadily defended the policy that had been adopted; but as he gradually came to see more clearly the serious difficulties and obstacles which must be encountered, and, if possible, overcome, in an extended scale of operations, he attached more value to an attack on the Helder and the capture of the Dutch fleet; and in his future conduct, as a War Minister, the instruction and experience which he then acquired produced a happy and beneficial influence on his policy. The views and projects of the Ministers with respect to the invasion of Holland by the combined forces of England and Russia, as well as the opinions of Sir Ralph, have now been unfolded as far and as accurately as the materials which were accessible permitted.

There is little to be told that can revive interest in the details of the short campaign in Holland. The ability and spirit with which the landing at the Helder was effected, and the uniform bravery displayed by the troops, are facts which have been universally recognised as honourable to the skill of the commander, and to the energy and dauntless courage of the English army. It is equally true that the rare quality of moral courage was never called into action under more painful circumstances than at the close of this campaign, when officers, who were ambitious of military fame, and who commanded a defeated but not dispirited army, found themselves compelled, by a strong and irresistible sense of public duty, to assent to a convention which they were well aware would wound the pride and damp the spirit of the country which they served.

The leading events of the campaign shall now be traced, not with the hope of throwing any new light on the military talents of Sir Ralph, but with the view of introducing such incidents as are illustrative of the motives which governed some important decisions, and are characteristic of Sir Ralph and of those with whom he had intimate relations.

The arrangements having been completed, 10,000 troops were embarked, and the fleet sailed with a fair wind on the 13th of August, under the command of Admiral Mitchell.

On the 14th, as has been already stated, Sir Ralph communicated to Admiral Mitchell his intention to make an attack on the Helder, and he instantly replied that he cordially approved of the decision, and that he would zealously co-operate with the army in the undertaking. On the following day, Sir Ralph having had an interview with the officer who had been sent to Lord Duncan, communicated to Mr. Dundas that nothing had occurred to alter his determination to proceed to the Helder—a decision of which Mr. Dundas expressed his most entire approval in a letter addressed to Sir Ralph on the 16th August. During the 13th and 14th, the wind continued to be favourable, but it was followed by most boisterous weather (very unusual at that season of the year). It was not until the 21st that the weather became propitious, and every preparation was then made for landing on the 22d; but again the weather became boisterous, and the fleet was obliged to put to sea. It was not until the evening of the 25th that the weather cleared up, and, on the 26th of August, the fleet came to anchor under the shore of the Helder, and the troops began to disembark at daylight on the 27th. During the delay occasioned by the adverse winds, the commanders adhered so steadily to their purpose, that they resolved not to abandon their intention of attacking the Helder, unless they should be compelled to do so by the want of water and provisions. On the 22d, General Brune, who commanded the united force of the French and Dutch Republics, was apprised of the real destination of the armament, and he instantly gave directions to General Daendels to proceed to North Holland

and assemble his division, which consisted of 4300 men, with six pieces of artillery, and which were already cantoned at Schlagenburg under General Van Guericke. On the 25th, General Daendels had collected a force between the Helder and Haarlem consisting of 10,300 men. From Huisduinen, near the Helder to the mouth of the Meuse, the coast of North Holland is bounded by a chain of sand-hills of various heights, and interrupted at intervals by openings towards the land. Between Huisduinen and Calandzoog the sand-hills rest on the basis of an ancient dyke, called Sand Dyke, at the foot of which the sands have gradually accumulated, and the shore between the hills and the sea is not more, in some places, than 1000 paces broad, and in others not more than 200. At three o'clock in the morning of the 27th, the boats, with the troops on board, were assembled, and began to move towards the shore. Some small armed vessels opened a brisk fire to clear the coast, under cover of which the troops, commanded by Sir James Pulteney, amounting to between 2000 and 2500 men, effected a landing. "Although," says Sir Ralph in his official despatch, " the enemy did not oppose our landing, yet the first division had scarcely begun to move forward before they got into action, which continued from five o'clock in the morning till three o'clock in the afternoon. The enemy had assembled a very considerable body of infantry, cavalry, and artillery, near Calandzoog, and made repeated attacks on our right with fresh troops. Our position was on a ridge of sand-hills stretching along the coast from north to south. Our right flank was unavoidably exposed to the whole fire of the enemy. We had nowhere sufficient ground on our right to form more than a battalion in line, yet, on the whole, the position, though singular, was not in our situation disadvantageous, having neither cavalry nor artillery. By the courage and perseverance of the troops, the enemy were fairly worn out, and obliged to retire in the evening to a position two leagues in their rear. The contest was arduous, and the loss has been considerable." Arrangements had been made for attacking the Helder, which contained a garrison of 2000 men, at daybreak of the morning of the 28th, " but about eight o'clock in the evening of the 27th, the Dutch fleet in the Nieuve Diep got under way, and the troops were withdrawn. About nine o'clock at night, General Moore took possession of that important post, in which he found a numerous artillery of the best kind, both of heavy and field train."

The numerical loss of the English in this action was 57 killed, of whom three were officers; 371 were wounded, of whom eighteen were officers; and 26 rank and file were missing. The loss of the enemy was greater than had been expected. General Daendels, in his official report, states that the action began early in the morning, and lasted till evening, having cost the loss in killed, wounded, and missing, of 1400 men, of whom fifty-seven were officers. It is possible, however, that in this statement, General Daendels may have included those who deserted. The effect of these operations was decisive as to the fate of the Dutch fleet, which was reduced to the alternative of surrendering to the Stadtholder or to the English. They chose the former alternative, and, on the 30th of August, they surrendered to the Stadtholder.

The complete success of these first operations, which secured the possession of the fort of the Helder and the Dutch fleet, did not alter the opinion which Sir Ralph had formed and expressed as to the ultimate result of the expedition in which he was embarked. He persevered zealously in the performance of his military duty, and he was supported by the consciousness that he had fulfilled his obligations to his country by having most unreservedly communicated his opinions to the Ministers. In writing to Mr. Dundas on 28th of August, the day after their first success, he says, "We have succeeded in our enterprise, which, as far as I can be allowed to judge, was most precarious, and which, if I am to give an opinion, ought not to have been risked. It is impossible as yet to form any opinion as to the disposition of the country. We shall observe strict order, and give every kind of protection to persons of all descriptions. We are now to make the most of our success, and as soon as we shall be enabled to procure horses and waggons, we shall endeavour to push on to Alkmaar, where the country becomes more cultivated and productive. As we have now a secure port, I hope there will be no delay in sending us three or four regiments of Light Dragoons, as the want of cavalry is sorely felt. The force that opposed us yesterday was about 7000 men, well clothed, well armed, and well disciplined. They may be said to have behaved better than we expected. They certainly at times pushed our people with spirit and perseverance, as they returned several times to the attack. I could not yesterday sufficiently admire the spirit of the British soldier. Without any sort of discipline, they did in their own way as much as could have been expected from veteran troops. Sir James Pulteney really surprised me. He showed ardour and intelligence, and did himself honour. I have reason to be satisfied with all the general officers, although they did not all show the same intelligence. Lieutenant-Colonel Hay, whom I highly valued, was killed by my side. He has left a widow and six daughters without a shilling. I trust that you will recommend Colonel Hay's family to the King's goodness. If I have endeavoured to render any service to the public on this occasion, the only reward that I ask is, that this poor family may not be left destitute."

On the same day on which Sir Ralph wrote to Mr. Dundas, he wrote a short letter to one of his own family, in which he says,—" This expedition has hung heavy on my mind ever since it was thought of. The risk was far too great, and now all is not daylight."

The success at the Helder was achieved under circumstances which added very materially to the perilous character of the undertaking. Many of the troops were raw, and, as Sir Ralph says, without discipline, and from the delay caused by adverse winds, a knowledge of the destination of the armament was acquired by the enemy in such time as enabled them to make preparations to meet the landing on the coast. If the weather had been such as was to be expected in the month of August, the landing might have been effected on the 19th, and before the point selected for attack was known to the enemy. Even if it had been effected on the 22d, as was at one time hoped would have been the case, the force assembled by the enemy would only have been 4300 instead of 7000, with which the British troops had to contend on the 27th; but although the delay caused by unfavourable weather was no doubt a serious disadvantage, the defenders of the expedition exaggerated its consequences when they represented it as the real source of the failure of the enterprise. The native valour of the English troops, the completeness and success of the arrangements made for their landing, and the confidence reposed both by officers and men in the experience and ability of the commander, overcame all difficulties.

In the letter which Sir Ralph wrote to Mr. Dundas, he did not mean to undervalue the importance of the success which had been achieved. The capture of the Dutch fleet, which he regarded as certain, was calculated to sustain the spirit of the English public, and if the expedition had then terminated, the disheartening failure which he anticipated from engaging in more extended operations would have been avoided. His object was to show that his own opinion remained unshaken, and he wished to repress those sanguine and, as he thought, unfounded hopes which would be raised by a first success. It was, perhaps, too much to expect that Ministers who were so deeply committed should consent to review their position after the surrender of the Dutch fleet; but if they had been wise enough then to pause, the lives of many brave men would have been saved, and an English army would not have been indebted for its safety to a humiliating convention.

On the evening of the 28th, a reinforcement under General Don, which had left England many days after the fleet, arrived at the Helder.

As soon as the English became masters of the Zuyder Zee, by the surrender of the Dutch ships of war, Sir Ralph determined to advance, but he was unable to do so until the 1st of September, from the difficulty of finding a sufficient number of horses to transport the subsistence of the troops which it was necessary to bring from the Helder. On that day Sir Ralph advanced with 12,000 men, leaving some troops in the Helder to protect and escort the stores and supplies, and took up a strong position at Potten, on the German Ocean, with his left at Oudersluys on the Zuyder Zee. This position was well chosen and strong, for enabling Sir Ralph to hold his ground securely until the Duke of York with the reinforcement from England, and the Russians, who were on the sea, should arrive. The strength of this position has been minutely described by an officer who served in Holland, and who has published an account of the campaign. His view was that the English object of the expedition having been accomplished by the surrender of the Dutch fleet, the position ought to have been fortified and left under the protection of a small force, while the rest of the English army crossed the Zuyder Zee, "instead of setting the English army, as the Ministers or Generals did, to fight their way to Amsterdam through the long defile of North Holland." This remark is only another proof of how rashly the expedition had been framed from its outset, for there is no doubt that the plan of operations on the Yssel had been maturely considered and rejected by the Ministers in England, because it would have been, in fact, the renewal of a Continental War, by sieges and battles, which was never contemplated by the projectors of the enterprise, who proposed, as is stated in the treaty with Russia, that an effort should be made to liberate Holland by a sudden attack, aided by the Dutch people, whom they supposed to be desirous to shake off the French yoke. At all events, it is plain that Sir Ralph was not one of the Generals who set the Army the hard task of forcing their way to Amsterdam through North Holland, as he thought the whole plan impracticable, although as a soldier he exerted all his energies to insure success and to maintain the honour of the English arms.

In pursuance of his instructions, Sir Ralph intrusted to General Don, a letter addressed to the Batavian Republic, and directed him to proceed to the head-quarters of General Daendels, and to apply for passports to enable him to execute his commission. General Daendels declined to decide the point, and referred it to General Brune, who refused to grant the passports, and General Don was obliged to return without having been able to execute his instructions. The enemy were aware that Sir Ralph was only holding his position until he received large reinforcements, and Sir Ralph, on his part, was fully prepared to expect that the enemy would be anxious to make an impression before the whole of the allied English and Russian forces were united. Accordingly, he had been vigilant and active in strengthening his position. The right was protected by an entrenchment, and by gunboats, stationed close to the shore. The left was the object of similar attention, as all the provisions from the Helder were landed there, and it was accordingly fortified with care. The intermediate points were judiciously strengthened, and every precaution had been adopted to insure success in repelling the anticipated attack. At daybreak, on the morning of the 10th of September, the enemy commenced an attack which was more particularly directed against the centre and right of the English force. The right column of the enemy, under General Daendels, attacked the village of St. Martin's, but not with much spirit. The main attacks were made by the Dutch troops, which composed the centre column of the enemy, and which marched on Krabbendam and De Zype, and by the left column, composed of French troops, which attacked the position of General Burrard, who commanded the second brigade of Guards. The enemy displayed great bravery and perseverance, but they were everywhere foiled by the strength of the position and the determined courage of the English troops. About ten o'clock the enemy retreated towards Alkmaar, leaving behind them many dead, some wounded, a piece of cannon, a number of waggons, pontoons, and portable bridges. The loss of the English was, thirty-seven rank and file killed, eleven officers, three serjeants, 131 rank and file wounded. The loss of the enemy in the two columns which were principally engaged was estimated at 1000 in killed and wounded.

The time was now come when Sir Ralph was to surrender the command to the Duke of York. He had executed with success the portion of the service that had been intrusted to him. The landing at the Helder, and the capture of that fort had been effected, a safe place of disembarkation had been secured for the English and Russian troops as they successively arrived, and he had occupied a strong position which he had been able to maintain against the assault of the enemy.

These successes caused general rejoicing in England. Mr. Dundas's own appreciation of the importance of the service rendered by Sir Ralph, and his recognition of the serious observations he had made before the expedition sailed, with regard to the difficulties to be encountered, are shown by the following extract from a private letter addressed to Sir Ralph, dated Walmer Castle, 3d September 1799 :—

"Your despatches reached me on Barham Downs this morning at ten o'clock. You will not expect me to detail to you my feelings of satisfaction on the present occasion; the service was the most important that could be performed, and it has been not only well, but completely done; there cannot be two opinions on that subject. Notwithstanding your opinion as to the danger of the attempt, you cannot expect me to say that I am sorry I preferred my own to your better judgment. Admiral Mitchell has completely kept his word with me. Your letters and his do honour to yourselves and to each other."

In another private letter from Mr. Dundas to Sir Ralph's eldest son, dated also from Walmer Castle, but written on the 6th of September 1799, he thus expresses himself:—

"You will naturally suppose how happy I am, both on public and private grounds, at the success which has attended this most important enterprise. Gratified as the country now is by the complete success, neither the Minister who planned, nor the General who executed, the enterprise, would have escaped censure if it had failed. In so far as I could, I took the responsibility on my shoulders. From what Sir Ralph stated to me, I was aware that risks were to be run, not justifiable by the rules of military prudence, and therefore, when I gave my last instructions, I expressly took the responsibility on myself. Thanks however to Heaven and to Sir Ralph, we stand on a pinnacle of glory and of fame. I cannot better convey to you what is felt on the subject than by transmitting to you a copy of my letter of thanks, dated 4th September 1799, which I have given to the Duke of York to deliver to Sir Ralph."

The public letter of thanks alluded to above by Mr. Dundas, as having been sent to Sir Ralph, contains the following expressions :—

"The anxiety in which His Majesty and the public had remained respecting the situation of the expedition under your command, was fortunately and most pleasingly relieved by the arrival of Major, now Lieutenant-Colonel Kempt, with your despatch of the 28th ultimo, which was immediately laid before the King. It is impossible for me to convey to you, in adequate terms, the sense His Majesty entertains of the steady and enterprising bravery of the army under your command in the arduous and ever-memorable action of the 27th ultimo. High as the character of the British Army stood before this event, it is impossible that the landing at the Helder point, preceded and attended by so many untoward difficulties, and the battle by which it was immediately followed, should not attract the admiration of Europe, and raise that character still higher in every part of the world, as it has done already in the eyes of their Sovereign and their countrymen at home.

"The cool judgment, military ardour, and superior abilities you have displayed on the occasion has justly drawn from His Majesty the warmest commendations. It is to these great qualities directing the enterprising courage of the troops, and to the able assistance of Lieutenant-General Sir James Pulteney, and the other general and staff officers engaged on the occasion, that His Majesty ascribes, under Providence, this brilliant opening of the campaign, and the important events by which it has been so rapidly improved."

On the same occasion the Corporation of the City of London conferred upon Sir Ralph their public thanks, together with the freedom of the city, and voted him a sword of the value of one hundred guineas.

Sir Ralph was naturally desirous that the command of an expedition, of which he thought unfavourably, should be, as speedily as possible, placed under the guidance of the commander to whom it was to be intrusted. But while he urged that the Duke of York should promptly assume the command, he gave the assurance that he would serve under His Royal Highness with as much constancy and zeal as if acting for himself,—a pledge which he most gallantly and honourably redeemed. It only remains to pass in review the fruitless display of valour, and the sacrifice of valuable lives which preceded the humiliating catastrophe of this ill-advised expedition.

The Duke of York landed at the Helder on the evening of the 13th of September, where he found that the first division of the Russians, under General Hermann, had already arrived, and they were followed in a few days by the second division. When the command of the united forces of England and Russia was intrusted to the Duke of York, it was arranged that on all important occasions reference should be made to the opinions of a council of war, to be composed of Sir David Dundas, Sir Ralph Abercromby, Sir James Pulteney, the Russian commander, and Lord Chatham. The force now placed under the command of the Duke of York amounted to thirty-three thousand men. The artillery were supplied with horses sent from England, but the commissariat and baggage were insufficiently provided with the means of rapid or continued movement. The Allies had, at first, a decided superiority in numbers, but that was the only advantage they possessed, as the enemy were daily increasing and concentrating their force, and were skilfully availing themselves of the means of defence which the country presented, and of the facilities which water carriage afforded for establishing magazines of military stores and provisions.

If there ever existed any real desire on the part of the Dutch people to co-operate with the Allies in an effort to re-establish the independence of their country, it was repressed by the balanced state of the war, and they invariably watched the course of events with sullen indifference. The Dutch troops had fought with bravery, and there had been few desertions. The people were sufficiently disposed to sell their produce for profit, but, in all other respects, they appeared to be listless spectators of the scene. The hereditary Prince of Orange had joined the army, where he was met by no indications of any support of an encouraging nature from the inhabitants, who, it is true, did not appear to be disposed, on the other hand, to assist the French, although they were daily increasing in number, and strengthening themselves in their position, and the season was advancing, which was favourable to them. On the whole, it must be admitted that the

Duke of York assumed the command under circumstances not merely unpromising, but which presented the most formidable difficulties.

The plan of the campaign, and the consequent operations, were regulated and directed by the Council of War. What part Sir Ralph took in the deliberations of the Council, and how far their decisions were sanctioned by his opinion, cannot now be known, as he always observed the strictest silence on that subject. It would perhaps not be uncandid to infer that he did not invariably concur in the decisions of the Council, as the only occasion on which he freely and voluntarily broke silence was with respect to the Convention, of which, however unpopular, he always took a large share of the responsibility. The Duke of York and his Council appear to have been of opinion, that as the season was far advanced, and the enemy were daily becoming stronger by the accessions to their number, and the increased strength of their positions, it was necessary that whatever was to be attempted should be done quickly. It was decided that a vigorous effort should be made in the hope that a brilliant success might open the way to Amsterdam. On the 19th of September an attack was made, and the army advanced in four columns. The left column under Sir Ralph marched on the evening of the 18th towards Hoorn, the object of this movement being to make a decisive impression in the event of the other columns being successful on the right of the enemy, which had been left somewhat exposed. The main attack was to be made by the Russians, who were to drive the enemy from the heights of Camperduyn, and finally to take possession of Bergen. The two centre columns were destined to co-operate with and to assist the main attack that was to be made by the Russians. It had been ordered that the attack should commence at daybreak, but two hours before that time a portion of the Russians advanced, and General Hermann, either because he felt that it was necessary to support those who had already marched forward, or being himself impatient to begin the action, caused a canal to be passed an hour before daylight, and commenced the attack on the entrenchments of the enemy. The Russians pressed forward with an energy and ardour that was irresistible, and they obtained a brief possession of Bergen, which was the object of the battle; but in achieving that success, all order and discipline were overthrown, and the French, profiting from the disorder of the assailants, rallied and repulsed them, taking General Hermann prisoner. The centre columns, which had obeyed orders, began the attack at the appointed time, and were in the course of effecting the duties assigned to them, but the defeat of the Russians rendered their efforts unavailing, and, after having given all the assistance in their power to their impetuous allies, they retired in good order.

Sir Ralph had taken possession of Hoorn, which he had been unable to reach until some hours after the appointed time, owing to the badness of the roads; and, after resting his troops, he was on the point of proceeding to execute the portion of the plan which had been intrusted to him, when he was informed of what had occurred on the right, and he was personally ordered to retire, as his advice was required without delay. The division returned without having been impeded by the enemy.

If this battle had been gained by the Allies, it may reasonably be doubted whether it would have been so decisive as to have realized the important results that were anticipated. It is very probable that, but for the impetuosity of the Russians, the event of the battle might have been different. They did succeed in obtaining a temporary possession of Bergen, but that success was achieved by a disobedience of orders in commencing the attack before the appointed time, at the risk of preventing the other columns from being ready at the proper moment to follow it up; and the want of discipline on the part of the Russians converted what had been a momentary success into a defeat. The loss of the English in this action was fifty officers and 1200 men, and that of the Russians at least 2000. The loss of the enemy must have been considerably less than that of the Allies. The capture of General Hermann, who was made prisoner, was severely felt. He was a brave and zealous, though perhaps not an experienced or skilful officer, and he was beloved by his troops. One inevitable consequence of this unfortunate battle was, that the Russians naturally endeavoured to excuse their own rashness, impetuosity, and disobedience of orders, by throwing the blame on their Allies for not supporting them. It is plain that there was not the slightest foundation for that charge, but the dislike and jealousy which, from that day, existed between the Russians and the English, added one more to the many difficulties to be encountered in this hopeless undertaking.

After the action of the 19th, the armies maintained the ground which they had respectively occupied, and General Brune having discovered the danger to which he had been exposed, of having his right turned by the Russians, and his rear attacked by the division under Sir Ralph, determined to strengthen his position. For this purpose he laid a portion of the country under water, and, by so doing, he was relieved from the necessity of defending, except by small detachments, the country between the Zuyder Zee and Alkmaar, and forced the Duke of York to make his attack in front. None of the difficulties which were to be encountered by the Allies had been overcome, but were, on the contrary, increased. The season had advanced, the enemy were strengthened, and all hopes of support or sympathy on the part of the Dutch people had vanished.

The position of the Duke of York had become perilous in the extreme. It was, however, determined to make one more effort, and the remainder of the month of September was employed by both armies in preparations for the coming conflict. It was not until the 2d of October that the Duke of York was enabled to make his great attack. On that day the army was divided into four columns, and to Sir Ralph the execution of the main attack was intrusted. The column under his command was directed to march along the shore, to turn the left flank of the enemy and to fall on their rear in case they persevered in attempting to maintain themselves in Bergen.

Another column, composed of Russians, under General Essen, who had succeeded General Hermann in the command, were to attack Bergen in front, while it was to be taken in reverse by Sir Ralph. A portion of the third column was to support General Essen, and the remainder to attack and carry Schoreldam. The fourth column, commanded by Sir James Pulteney, was to threaten the enemy's right, and to be kept in reserve to take advantage of such favourable opportunities as might occur. By this arrangement the two wings were composed of English, and the two centre columns of Russian and English troops. After very considerable efforts the enemy were driven from the sandhills on the coast, and if General Essen could have been prevailed upon to have advanced on Bergen, the French column, which was retiring and almost turned, might have been cut off. The column under Sir David Dundas was too weak to attack Bergen alone, having been unable to bring the artillery over the sandhills, and was therefore obliged to be satisfied with maintaining the ground that had been gained. If the success of the column under Sir Ralph had been seconded by cordial co-operation on the part of General Essen, and by an effective execution of the duty intrusted to him, the results of the action would have been more important, as will appear from the public despatch of the Duke of York, who thus describes the progress of the column commanded by Sir Ralph:—"The main body of Sir Ralph Abercromby's column had proceeded without meeting much resistance in the early part of the day, but was, nevertheless, much inconvenienced, and his troops harassed by the necessity of detaching continually into the sandhills to his left to cover that flank against the troops whom the enemy had placed on them. The admirable disposition, however, which he made of his troops, and their determined spirit and gallantry, enabled him to arrive within a mile of Egmont. Here he was seriously opposed by a considerable corps of French infantry which occupied Egmont-op-Zee, and the high sandhills in its front, and who had formed a very strong corps of cavalry and artillery on the beach. The engagement was maintained during several hours with the greatest obstinacy, and in no instance were the abilities of a commander, or the heroic perseverance of troops more highly conspicuous. Animated by the example of Sir Ralph Abercromby, and the general and other officers under him, the troops sustained every effort made upon them by an enemy their superior in numbers and much favoured by the strength of their position." On this occasion Sir Ralph had two horses shot under him.

The Duke of York in this despatch very correctly described the feeling of the Army with respect to the ability of the commander and the bravery of the troops, displayed in the battle at Egmont, which was generally regarded as not only the most distinguished, but as the redeeming event in the campaign in Holland. An intercepted letter, written during the action by General Borstel to General Vandamme, who did not join the army till near the close of the action, throws light on the events of the day, and on the motive which urged the French to make so persevering a resistance at Egmont. General Borstel expresses the greatest alarm for the fate of the French column which was in imminent danger of being either cut off or wholly routed if General Essen had advanced on Bergen, as he was pressed to have done. The object, therefore, of making such an obstinate resistance at Egmont, was to give time to the French column to retreat. The result of the action was that the Allies remained in possession of the field of battle, and the enemy abandoned the positions they had occupied as well as an extent of country which, under ordinary circumstances, might have been regarded as an adequate reward of victory; but although the enemy retired it was only to occupy positions still stronger than those which they had abandoned, and to receive large reinforcements which were hastening to join them. The force of the Allies had sustained an additional loss of 2000 men in killed and wounded, and the liberation of Holland was as distant and hopeless as ever. At each succeeding stage in the progress of the expedition the same difficulty presented itself—How to persevere with any reasonable hope of success, or how to retire without discredit. It is not surprising that a young Prince placed at the head of the Allied force, should be desirous to persevere as long as there existed even a ray of hope. It is not surprising that the Council which had been appointed to assist the Duke of York in carrying into execution a plan which had been adopted by England and by Russia, should be slow to incur the responsibility of abandoning the expedition at the moment when the enemy appeared to have sustained a defeat. The consequence was, that it was determined that another effort should be made.

On the 6th of October, the Duke of York pushed forward the advanced posts of his right and centre, with a view of securing for the different columns points of departure more free and nearer to the enemy, when he should make the general attack for which he was then preparing. At first this movement was made without difficulty, and without threatening to involve any other consequences than those which had been anticipated. The Russians wishing to strengthen their position pushed on beyond the limits that had been prescribed, and the enemy, not doubting that a general attack was intended on their position, reinforced their advanced guard, and gradually a general action ensued, contrary to the intention of both parties. At nightfall the French retired, and left the Allies in possession of the post for which they had been contending. The details of such a conflict would be devoid of all interest, although it was very bloody, and its consequences decided the fate of the expedition. The loss of the Allies in this action was not less than two thousand five hundred men, of whom about seven hundred were prisoners.

This unexpected action extinguished all hope of being able to make such an impression on the enemy as would justify farther perseverance in the enterprise. Under this impression Sir Ralph

Abercromby, Sir David Dundas, and Sir James Pulteney, signed a paper, which they delivered to the Duke of York, and in which they assigned their reasons for recommending His Royal Highness to retreat to the position of the Zype, and there to wait for instructions from England. The Generals represented to His Royal Highness that in the five actions in which the Army had been engaged, their loss, on the whole, amounted to between nine and ten thousand men, which could not be easily replaced, while the enemy, whose loss had not been less considerable, had received and were receiving large reinforcements; they enumerated the various difficulties which had impeded the transport of provisions and supplies, and they stated that the position which the Army occupied afforded no natural advantages, and could not be improved by art, and that even if they gained the position of Beverwyk, they could not maintain it, as they possessed no certain means for the conveyance of provisions, and that they would have the formidable French Army in their front, and the greatest part of the Dutch troops on the left flank and in the rear. Finally, they submitted to His Royal Highness that the expedition had been undertaken in the hope that the Dutch people would join heartily in an effort for their own liberation, and that the French being pressed on the most vulnerable points of their frontiers would be unable to defend those that were more distant and less important, but that both these expectations had been signally disappointed, as there had been no movement on the part of the Dutch, and the French had been able to reinforce their army in Holland to an extent that rendered the prosecution of the enterprise hopeless. This reasoning was conclusive, and amply justified the opinions of those who predicted failure in a protracted effort for the expulsion of the French, and the restoration of the independence of Holland.

In compliance with the advice of the three Generals, the Duke of York, on the morning of the 7th of October, began to draw off his army, with the view of re-occupying their former position of the Zype. This object was accomplished without loss, as the roads had been so much cut up and damaged, that the enemy were unable to harass them in their retreat.

On the 9th of October, the Duke of York informed the Ministers of his return to the position of the Zype, and applied for further instructions. Sir Ralph, at the same time, addressed the following letter to Mr. Huskisson :—" *Schagenburg, October*

10, 1799.—Colonel Brownrigg, who goes to England with the Duke's despatches, will fully explain to you our situation, and will show to Mr. Dundas a paper signed by myself, Sir David Dundas, and Sir James Pulteney, in which we give some of the principal reasons why we thought it advisable to resume the position of the Zype. It is impossible to conceal from the most short-sighted the situation in which we are placed. I need not, therefore, point it out to you. What depends on us shall be done; the position is good, the army still numerous, and the troops not defeated. It is impossible, however, that we can remain here long; the means of subsistence must fail, and our wants must increase. Should the enemy press on us, we must once more attack him, but to advance into the country is impracticable.

"From the moment of our arrival, orders were given to fortify the Helder, but the means of execution have been few, and no great progress has been made, and it will now be expedient to forward, with every possible exertion, the fortifications. But, above all, you must seriously consider what you are to do with an army of 24,000 men, cooped up in a corner of an impracticable country. I am unwilling to write to Mr. Dundas on the subject; my mind always went in opposition to the undertaking, and I spoke my sentiments on it so fully before I left England, that it is decent to be silent in my correspondence with him, or the consequences likely to result from it. We are certainly unfortunate in our Russian Allies. The less, however, that is said on that head the better; we must endeavour to keep them in good humour, and there are no such means as giving them meat and drink. It has been recommended to the Duke to give them something in lieu of bat and forage money, an allowance for horses, and a proportion of meat to the men.

"I much doubt if any attempt on Friesland or Groningen is either practicable or expedient. As yet, the Army is not sickly, but sickness must necessarily come. As to myself, I do not sleep on a bed of roses. I feel deeply interested for the young Prince who commands, and it is my anxious wish to be useful to him in any shape. I should not be pardonable if I omitted mentioning, in the fullest manner, the abilities and heroism of General Moore. I have seen so much of his conduct, that I can speak confidently. To him you may safely look as a most promising officer; he goes to England, covered with honourable scars, and were I King of England I should administer a salve."

Before Colonel Brownrigg could have returned from England, and before any fresh instructions could have been received by the Duke of York, a negotiation had been opened with General Brune. A few brief passages in the letters written by Sir Ralph at this time to one of his own family throw light on the negotiation, and on his opinions and conduct at this important crisis. On the 20th of October, he writes: "We have entered into an agreement to withdraw the Allied Army from Holland on or before the 30th of November, and to restore to France and Holland 8000 prisoners. An armistice has taken place. What do you think of this? I have given my consent, but I do not consider that this convention gives us any security. The contracting parties are the Duke of York, Admiral Mitchell, and General Brune." On the 31st of October, Sir Ralph again writes: "I wrote to you on the signing of the Convention. What could tempt the French to agree to it, I cannot conceive. One-half of this Army must have fallen into their hands, with all our artillery, stores, etc. It would have overset the Ministry, so great would have been the indignation of the nation, however ill directed. I am sure they ought to thank the Duke of York for listening to the advice which he got on this occasion. Whether our conduct is approved or not, is to me a matter of indifference, being conscious that we were in the right. The first hint came from the French Army, which was taken up by the Duke's Etat-Major; when proposed by them to me, I desired them to put it down in writing. I heartily concurred with them, and desired them to carry it to Lord Chatham, which was done. As to the number of prisoners to be returned, whether 5000 or 8000, it appeared to be of no great importance. The chief objects were not to commit, by any act of ours, the Ministry, and not a word to be allowed to be said about the Fleet. All inferior articles were left to be adjusted by General Brune and General Knox. The agreement has been ratified, hostages have mutually been given, and more than two-thirds of the Anglo-Russian Army are embarked. It would not now be worth while to break from the Armistice for so small an object.

"A great change has taken place in the manners of the French since 1794. They are more perfectly civilized; they have not exactly the tone of the old system, but more frankness and apparent candour. Nothing can exceed the humanity that has been practised between the rival nations."

In writing to Mr. Dundas, on the 26th of October, Sir Ralph thus expresses himself:—

"It has apparently suited the convenience of the French Directory to sanction the Armistice. We shall get off with some difficulty, and not without risk, from the badness of the port of the Helder, and the inclemency of the weather. With a superior army in our rear, it is difficult to see how the Army would have got off, especially as the works ordered at the Helder, on my arrival, had been long neglected, and are in a very imperfect state. Whatever may be the opinion of others, I shall boldly set my face to the Convention signed by the Duke, and when the welfare of an army is at stake, one cannot allow feelings and such unmeaning words to have any weight. If an army were so situated as to be able to open a way with their swords, any agreement might have been a disgrace, but that was not the case. The army you sent to Holland will return with the real loss of three or four thousand British. Many of the wounded and sick will rejoin their regiments. In the spring you will have a fine army if the brigades are put under major-generals who are capable of instructing young officers and training soldiers. They must remain stationary, and not be allowed to dance all over Great Britain. I have been cautious in blaming the Russians. I must, however, acknowledge that I have seen nothing to admire. I am sensible of the great exertions made to send a considerable force to Holland. So much is wanting to enable an army to act, that unless we could have kept our ground during the winter, we could not have hoped to be in an active state till spring. From apathy this country seems contented under its present governors. I have not seen anything like opposition, and there have been no acts of cruelty as far as I have heard. The hereditary Prince of Orange is the most ungracious, weak prince in Europe. Except one man from Hoorn, no person has come near him, or had any communication with him. He knows as little of the country as if he had been born in Sweden. He is not a man whom you can support from any motive of personal character. My further services are not worth offering. I am not, however, discouraged; and I have but one wish in this world,—the honour and welfare of the country."

A disastrous conclusion to the enterprise had been clearly foreseen by Sir Ralph, who, in a private letter dated on the 30th of September, had endeavoured to prepare the public for such a result. He then wrote:—

"Our situation does not improve; the weather is bad, the enemy gain strength from inundations, and they fortify every other point. The Russians, *entre nous*, seem to be a strange kind of people. There may be bravery, but there is no discipline. The general may cane an officer, but he does not prevent plunder and robbery. Our people have behaved uncommonly well in that respect. We must expect sickness from the climate and the weather, and I wish the nation may prepare itself for a disappointment. If the expedition had ended with the surrender of the Dutch fleet, everybody would have been satisfied. In short, my reason does not tell me that we are to have any success. Perhaps those who are better informed have a right to see things in a different point of view."

In reply to the letter of Sir Ralph, sent by Colonel Brownrigg, Mr. Huskisson wrote what follows, which is important, as containing his views of the campaign in Holland :—

"I cannot allow Colonel Brownrigg to return to head-quarters without thanking you for your letter of the 10th, and expressing how much, on every ground, public and private, I feel gratified at your having, without accident, borne so principal and distinguished a share in the gallant but bloody conflicts our Army has so honourably sustained in Holland. Being at present very much taken up in preparing the despatches to be forwarded by Brownrigg to his Royal Highness, I cannot enter into a view of your situation. I own, considering the season, the importance of not totally ruining our Army, the apathy of the Dutch, and the efforts of the French, I have wished, since the attack of the 19th, that the campaign had ended with the brilliant *coup-de-main* that gave us the fleet. That battle opened my eyes on several points, and I believe others saw things as I did, but they are naturally over sanguine. Perhaps in the Army itself this was too much the case, and, if so, their confidence, and, above all, their extreme good conduct, justified the brilliant expectations of those who were anxiously watching the course of events at home. I really believe it was a gratifying circumstance to Mr. Dundas to be enabled, with the concurrence of the Duke of York, to recommend to the King to desist from the prosecution of the campaign, and to bring back the troops to this country. He feels, as you do, most anxious for the glory and the safety of his Royal Highness, and, if possible, his conduct during this short campaign has rendered his character more dear to him than it was before he left England.

"When I venture to mention a military subject, I have no excuse but anxiety for a successful issue to your arrangements for the embarkation of the army. In the presence of an enemy flushed with success in every quarter, and receiving daily reinforcements, it must be a most arduous and complicated operation. I trust there is no reason to apprehend a disaster, but I shall certainly be upon thorns until it has taken place.

"The manner in which you mention General Moore, whom you have taught me to admire, induced me, among other reasons, which you will collect from this letter, to communicate yours to Mr. Dundas."

This calm, candid, and able letter of Mr. Huskisson, shows how sanguine had been the hopes of the projectors of the expedition, how long they were cherished, and how unpalatable the objections, dictated by experience and knowledge, must have been. Mr. Huskisson acknowledges that the results of the action of the 19th opened his eyes to the reality of the case, and that even Mr. Dundas was secretly rejoiced that the means, however painful, of withdrawing the Army had been found.

The letter which Mr. Dundas wrote to Sir Ralph on the same occasion, is characteristic of his courage and fortitude under the pressure of the most discouraging circumstances. He writes, "I have received your letter by the messenger Scott, and Huskisson has communicated to me your letter to him. I hope it will not be long before I see you, to enter into all the ideas contained in your letter. If I had foreseen, that in the month of August you were to have had a hurricane, and in the months of September and October a deluge, I probably should not have ordered the armament to sail at the time I did. I give, however, a cordial approbation to the conduct of the Duke of York in retreating the Army to the strong position they had before the 2d, and I have as little doubt in advising his Majesty, in the letter I have this moment written to him, to give immediate directions for bringing the troops from Holland. But I wish you not to understand from this, that, upon a full review of all that has happened, I in any respect repent of anything that has been ordered by me. If the thing was to do again, and I was certain, that with all the loss we have suffered, the result was to be the capture of the Dutch Fleet, I would order the armament to sail. I say so, taking into calculation all the hurricanes and all the deluges that have obstructed us. But surely, taking the subject in that point of view, I at least argue the point fairly with those who differ from me, for they are not at liberty to employ arguments founded on hurricanes in August, and deluges in September and October, upon neither of which is anybody entitled to count.

"I therefore desire, that none of you will return with heads hanging down in despair, or as if you were returning as condemned criminals. I hold you up in a very different tone, and I have the satisfaction to feel the country does the same. In short, Colonel Brownrigg will tell you all I have said to him, and probably the Duke of York will show you the letter I wrote to him. Bring me back as many good troops as you can, and before next spring I will show you an Army the country never saw before. How to dispose of them must depend on circumstances at the moment."

The circumstances which have now been detailed, have clearly established the fact, that Sir Ralph never encouraged the effort that was made for the liberation of Holland, and that he firmly and perseveringly protested against it. It is true that the object professed by the framers of the treaty with Russia, was, that Holland was to be liberated by a sudden attack, aided by the efforts of the Dutch people. Sir Ralph was well aware that a sudden attack was impossible, on account of the time that was required to make the necessary preparations, and on account of the difficulties inseparable from the perils of a maritime expedition on a great scale. He foresaw, that if the attempt was made, it must end in a protracted campaign, for which our means were insufficient. He saw that the note of preparation had raised the hopes of the nation, which it would have been unwise to have wholly disappointed. He therefore fixed on the attack on the Helder as the only practicable way of avoiding disappointment, and sustaining the spirit of the people, and the instructions given to him show that the more the object of the expedition was considered, the more the difficulties of conducting extended operations were felt, and the more the advantage of directing our efforts, at least in the first instance, to the accomplishment of a success that would be gratifying to the English people, was appreciated. When the Helder and the Dutch fleet had been captured, Sir Ralph cautioned the Ministers not to be carried away by this first success, and he made them aware that it had in no degree shaken the opinions which he had expressed.

Throughout the campaign, he was under the impression that the result would be unfavourable, if not disastrous, but that feeling did not weaken or impair the zeal with which he exerted himself in a hopeless service, and when the final catastrophe came, he devoted himself with, if possible, increased ardour in his efforts to save the Army, and he freely and unreservedly took on himself a very large share of the responsibility for the Convention that was made.

The French Directory having ratified the Convention, no time was lost in re-embarking the troops and retiring from Holland.

Sir Ralph, attended by his personal staff, embarked and landed at Shields, and went direct to Scotland, to resume the command of the forces, which had been held during his absence by General de Burgh, the general officer next in rank. The opinion prevailed very generally among the public, that Sir Ralph had disapproved of the expedition to Holland, and the circumstance of his returning to Scotland without having communicated with the Ministers on events in which he had acted so prominent a part, was regarded as a confirmation of it. The Ministers were disappointed that Sir Ralph did not go to London; but, as he could not defend an undertaking of which he had disapproved, and did not wish to give public expression to his real opinions, he very naturally at once resumed his command and rejoined his family.

The humiliating result of this expedition necessarily gave rise to debates in Parliament, in which the opponents of Ministers assumed as a fact, though without any proof which they could produce, that Sir Ralph had throughout disapproved of the enterprise. The Ministers did not venture to assert that he had approved of the expedition, but they fixed on a detached sentence in one of his letters, which, taken by itself, seemed to hold out a prospect of success; while, from the context, it was plain that it was thrown out as the only possible event that could afford the slightest encouragement to the Duke of York, to sustain him in the arduous and perilous command which he was about to assume. When Sir Ralph complained that a partial quotation of a single passage in one of his letters, had given an unfounded and unwarrantable impression of his opinions, the most conciliatory and apologetic explanations were liberally offered. In truth, Mr. Dundas, to whom the letter was addressed, from which the quotation was made, was perfectly aware that the event to which Sir Ralph had referred as possible, was only pointed out to prevent the Duke of York from being depressed and discouraged in the execution of the service, to the performance of which he was irretrievably committed.

Although the Ministers may at times have been

vexed and even offended by the freedom with which Sir Ralph criticised their projects when they were submitted to his consideration, and by the unreserved expression of his opinions, they were nevertheless just towards him, and highly appreciated his services, as will appear from the following correspondence relative to the offer of a peerage which was made to him, and which he declined. On the 10th of October, Mr. Dundas wrote to the Duke of York, that "At the time the news arrived of the success of the Army at the Helder, and the subsequent capture of the Dutch fleet, Mr. Pitt observed to me, that no such brilliant service had been performed during the war, or perhaps any war, without receiving a distinguished mark of His Majesty's approbation, and he mentioned his wish of carrying to His Majesty his opinion that a peerage should be conferred on Sir Ralph Abercromby, which he considered to be the more necessary as so many distinctions of that nature had been conferred on naval services, but none in the course of the war upon services by His Majesty's land forces. I, however, thought it right, after what Mr. Pitt had said, to report the conversation to Sir Ralph, which I did by a letter a few days after, and I enclose an extract from his answer." The enclosed extract was: "I must deprecate a title either for myself or any of my family. Allow us to go on in the paths of industry in our different pursuits." In the meanwhile, the Duke of York had anticipated the letter from Mr. Dundas, to whom he had, on the 4th of October, addressed the following letter, after the action in which Sir Ralph distinguished himself at Egmont:—" What I have much at heart is, that this opportunity should be taken of showing some mark of His Majesty's approbation to Sir Ralph Abercromby. I know his delicacy about accepting a peerage. It is for you to consider how far his own feelings ought to be consulted, when certainly it would be a compliment to the Army. The action was fought between Bergen and Egmont. Sir Ralph Abercromby was engaged at Egmont; that, therefore, would certainly be the title most complimentary to himself. Should, however, any difficulties arise on account of the Egmont family, may I say, that I should consider it as a favour done to me if he was to receive the title of Bergen." Mr. Dundas forwarded the preceding correspondence to the King, accompanied with the following note:—" Mr. Dundas humbly transmits to your Majesty the accompanying correspondence with his Royal Highness the Duke of York for your Majesty's perusal and consideration. Independently of his general feeling of duty as an officer and a good subject, Mr. Dundas has personally reason to know that no reward he could ever receive, no distinction that could be conferred on him, would give Sir Ralph Abercromby half the satisfaction he derives from every opportunity afforded to him of proving the high sense of gratitude he feels from the generous support your Majesty and the Duke of York administered to him on his last return from Ireland, a time when every support was necessary to protect him from the unprincipled faction that was then combined against him. Mr. Pitt has never said so to Mr. Dundas, but he cannot help thinking that part of Mr. Pitt's anxiety to mark Sir Ralph on this occasion, may arise from his recollection of some circumstances that occurred at that time." Eventually his Majesty acquiesced in the refusal of the peerage by Sir Ralph, but suggested that as he had served in the West Indies, it would be a reason for giving him a grant of Carib lands, and he added, "I am not surprised Mr. Pitt feels that Sir Ralph was not justly treated in Ireland. I know he has a heart, when he has had time for reflection, that ever inclines him to judge equitably."

A rumour having reached Sir Ralph that there

was an intention to act on the suggestion of the King, with respect to a grant of Caribbean lands, he, on the 30th of November 1799, addressed the following letter to Mr. Dundas :—" It has been hinted to me that in consideration of the services I may have done in the way of my profession I am to receive a grant of Caribbean lands, or a sum of money arising from them. If it is thought that I am deserving of any mark of public favour, it is from the public alone that I can receive it. I am not a beggar or a covetous person to ask private honours or private grants. Good God, sir, what opinion should I have of myself were I to profit from the crimes and forfeitures of such a set of miscreants as the Caribs! I hope I shall trouble you no more on my services or their rewards. As long as my mind and body remain entire, I am bound to the service of my country."

Some weeks after the preceding letter had been written, Mr. Dundas happened to be in Scotland, and he placed the correspondence relative to the peerage in the hands of Sir Ralph, who returned it with the following note :—

"EDINBURGH, *January* 30, 1800.

" I beg leave to return you many thanks for the communication of the enclosures, and for the conversation you allowed me an opportunity to hold with you yesterday. I should be happy if I could persuade myself that Mr. Pitt now thinks more favourably of my conduct in Ireland. If I ever thought well of myself, if I ever thought that I had deserved well of the public, it was during my short command in that country. Lord Camden, thinking in private as I did, had not the courage to act as he ought; he had not the generosity to do me justice; he had the weakness to injure me with Mr. Pitt."

There is no doubt whatever, as was well known to those who possessed his confidence, that in declining a peerage Sir Ralph was governed by the high standard by which he estimated fame. He was unwilling that his name should be permanently associated with a service of which the result had been so humiliating to the country. Mr. Pitt proposed that the peerage should be conferred in consideration of the brilliant attack on the Helder, and the capture of the Dutch fleet, and if it had then been promptly offered, it is possible that it might not have been refused, as Sir Ralph felt that the service then rendered had been both useful and honourable to the country. The prominent part which Mr. Pitt took with respect to the peerage is honourable to him, as he overcame the unfavourable impression that had been made with respect to the conduct of Sir Ralph in Ireland.

It may be remarked that Sir Ralph, in writing to Mr. Dundas, on the 30th of January 1800, expresses himself in more unfavourable terms with respect to the personal conduct of Lord Camden, than he had done in the letters written while he was in Ireland. It was not until Sir Ralph returned from Ireland to London that he was fully aware of the impression that had been made by Lord Camden on the mind of Mr. Pitt, which sufficiently accounts for the resentment which he felt against the uncandid and unjust conduct of the Lord-Lieutenant.

Sir Ralph was gratified by finding that Mr. Pitt had been led by reflection, and by more correct information, to do him justice. He always rated highly the abilities of Mr. Pitt, of whom his judgment is expressed in a letter which he wrote to his eldest son, who had met Mr. Pitt for the first time. Sir Ralph says,—" In Mr. Pitt you gained an agreeable companion at table, and you saw in him very nearly a great man in the Cabinet. If his mind was equal to his abilities and talents, he would deserve the name of a first-rate statesman. Be that as it may, we are obliged to him, as we may doubt whether there is any one better fitted for his station."

Sir Ralph remained in Scotland until he was called upon to engage in the service in which he closed his life.

CHAPTER VI.

EXPEDITION AGAINST CADIZ.

1800.

ON the 22d of April 1800, Sir Ralph Abercromby, who was then in Edinburgh, received a summons from Mr. Dundas, Secretary of State for the War Department, requiring his immediate presence in London. On the following day, Sir Ralph took leave of his family, and left Scotland, never to return.

On arriving in London Sir Ralph was informed that a plan for co-operation with the Austrians in Italy had been submitted to the Government by General Sir Charles Stuart, to whom the conduct of the intended enterprise had been intrusted. The object of the plan was to take possession of the Maritime Alps, with the view of cutting off the communication between France and Italy. This plan was then abandoned in consequence of an alarm that a Spanish army, supported by the French, was about to invade Portugal, and accordingly fresh instructions were sent to Sir Charles Stuart, who, either from disapproving the change of plan, or from some other cause, suddenly resigned the command.

The Portuguese had, in the meanwhile, applied to England for aid, and had asked that Sir Ralph should be sent to take the command of their army. This proposal was submitted by Mr. Dundas to Sir Ralph, who said, that as he had expressed his willingness to serve so long as he could be useful, he should not object to go to Portugal to report on the state of the Portuguese army, and the means which the country possessed to resist the attack with which it was threatened, but beyond that he could not promise to go.

Mr. Dundas, taking a sanguine view of Sir Ralph's reply, assured his colleagues that he would accept the command of the Portuguese army; but when the subject was again discussed, Sir Ralph stated that he never intended to consent to transfer his services to another sovereign, and never would do so, but that, in the event of war, and of English co-operation being afforded to Portugal on an adequate scale, he would be willing to command both armies. The threatened invasion of Portugal proved, however, to be a false alarm, and the subject dropped.

Sir Ralph had at various times represented to Mr. Dundas, that he was now advanced in years, and that it was important for the public interests that younger officers should be brought forward, and he had pointed out Sir Charles Stuart as one who, from his rank and abilities, was well qualified to take a prominent place in the military service of the country. This suggestion had been acted upon, but on General Sir Charles Stuart's voluntary resignation, Sir Ralph, although in the sixty-sixth year of his age, did not hesitate to accept the command in the Mediterranean, which was represented as likely to become both urgent and important.

The necessary arrangements having been completed with all possible despatch, Sir Ralph, on the 12th May 1800, repaired to Portsmouth, and on the 13th embarked on board the "Sea-horse" frigate, and after various delays from adverse winds, arrived in Gibraltar Bay on the 6th of June. After a short stay at Gibraltar, Sir Ralph proceeded to Minorca, to assume the command to which he had been appointed.

Previous to the opening of the campaign of this

year, a plan of operations had been agreed upon between the English and Austrian Cabinets, by which it was provided that 10,000 British troops should be sent to co-operate with the Austrians in Italy. Early in March, a portion of the force destined for this service, had been sent to the Mediterranean, and Sir Charles Stuart, as has already been stated, had been appointed to the command; the resignation of that officer, and the false alarm as to the invasion of Portugal by the Spaniards, led to the decision, that the troops which had not yet been embarked for the Mediterranean should be countermanded. Under these altered circumstances, the instructions given to Sir Ralph were, to effect landings at different points on the coast of Italy, in order to draw off the attention of the French from the Austrian army under the command of General Melas, and to use all means that could be devised to accelerate the surrender of Malta, which was closely blockaded.

Sir Ralph found at Minorca a disposable force of 6000 men, and, having received an application from General Melas to send a reinforcement to strengthen Genoa, which had surrendered to the Austrians, he immediately sailed for that place, leaving orders for 4000 men to be sent after him with the greatest possible expedition. A few hours after Sir Ralph had sailed from Minorca, a despatch was received from Lord Keith, announcing that Bonaparte had crossed the Alps, broken into the Milanese, and gained the signal and decisive battle of Marengo.

General Fox, who commanded at Minorca, thinking that he had no authority to detain the troops, allowed the embarkation to proceed as directed. In the meanwhile, Sir Ralph having been apprised of the event which had occurred, altered his course, and he, with these troops, joined the English fleet then at Leghorn, where both Lord Keith and Lord Nelson had their flags flying. Sir Ralph went on board Lord Keith's ship, where he was made acquainted with the details of the battle of Marengo and its consequences. General Melas, who had retreated behind the Mincio, there to await orders from his Court, represented that he was still in a condition to renew hostilities, and in this opinion he was supported by Lord William Bentinck, who was attached to the Austrian army.

For the present nothing was to be done, but Sir Ralph subsequently despatched General Hope, and Colonel Lindenthal, an Austrian by birth, who was on Sir Ralph's personal staff, to General Melas, not only to ascertain the real state of the Austrian army, but with power to agree with him upon any reasonable plan of co-operation on the part of the British. The report made by these officers showed that no such plan could be formed, and, therefore, that the first part of Sir Ralph's instructions to co-operate with the Austrians, had clearly become impracticable.

The Queen of Naples, who had fled on the approach of the French, was also at this time at Leghorn. Her Majesty pressed Sir Ralph to undertake the defence of Naples, but he, well knowing the insufficiency of his own means, and aware that no reliance could be placed on the Neapolitan army, declined the proposal. Her Majesty urged her request with the impetuosity and intemperance which so strongly marked her character, but Sir Ralph was firm, and he finally said, " that, without positive orders from his own Court, compliance on his part was impossible." Sir Ralph ordered the troops which had reached Leghorn, to return to Minorca, and he sailed for Malta, with the intention of carrying into effect the second part of his instructions, which required him to use all such means as he could devise to facilitate the surrender of that island, and, this object having been accomplished,

Sir Ralph returned to Minorca, where he arrived on the 2d of August.

The disposable troops under the command of Sir Ralph were kept quite distinct from the garrison of Minorca, under the command of General Fox; and, on the morning of the 10th of August, Sir Ralph began a minute inspection of them, and, on finishing it on the 15th, expressed his entire approbation of their general appearance, and remarked that he observed among them many young soldiers well worthy of every care and attention, and particularly recommended those of that class to the generals and other officers, adding that the time might come when their own honour and the glory of their country might depend upon their exertions.

Such details are minute, but they mark the unremitting zeal of a commander who omitted no opportunity to enforce on the generals and other officers the most careful and exact performance of their duty towards those over whom they were placed, and to inspire all with a spirit which subsequently enabled them to display at the landing in Egypt, and on its sandy shores, a union of bravery, discipline, and ardour, which realized the prophetic words of Sir Ralph, " that the time might come when their own honour, the glory of their country," and, it might have been added, the peace of Europe, " would depend on their exertions."

On the 24th of August, Sir Ralph received instructions to effect a landing at Cadiz, to seize on the arsenals of the Caraccas, to destroy the docks, naval stores, and as many of the ships as possible; but the same instruction proceeded to state, that as it was not wished that much risk should be run, he was pointedly ordered not to land, unless he was confident that he should be able to re-embark and bring off the troops.

Orders were immediately issued for the embarkation of the troops, and on the 31st of August the fleet sailed from Minorca for Gibraltar, where, after much stormy weather, they arrived on the 13th September, and were joined on the 19th by the troops under the command of Sir James Pulteney.

At this season of the year, Gibraltar could not furnish a sufficient supply of water for so large a fleet, and the anchorage being deemed unsafe, the greater number of the ships were sent to Tetuan. Sir Ralph and Sir James Pulteney remained at Gibraltar to make the necessary arrangements for the services with the conduct of which they were respectively intrusted. The whole force embarked consisted of 20,000 infantry, 772 artillery, and 200 cavalry, making a total of 20,972 men. The Army was divided into two wings, the right being under the command of General Hutchinson, and the left under that of Sir James Pulteney.

Before entering on the detail of the unfortunate failure of the expedition to Cadiz, it is necessary to revert to the tenor of the instructions received by Sir Ralph, with regard to the precautions to be observed in the event of an attempt to land being decided on. The certainty required by these instructions could only be obtained in the event of there being such safe anchorage for the Fleet as would insure constant communication, a regular supply of stores and provisions, and the means of bringing off the troops. These were naval questions, which it was necessary to submit to the decision of the Admiral. If it was clear that the certainty required by the instructions could not be obtained, the enterprise ought not to be attempted. Accordingly, Sir Ralph prepared his plan, and submitted it to Lord Keith before the Fleet left Gibraltar. The General proposed to land the troops at Rota, about six leagues to the northward of Cadiz, and that his first object should be to seize Santa Catalina, under the impression that between these two points, which form part of the Bay, the Fleet could lie at anchor in tolerable safety; and to this plan Lord Keith assented.

The Fleet sailed from Gibraltar upon this understanding between the naval and military commanders. On the 2d of October, the Fleet passed through the Straits, arriving off Cadiz on the evening of the 3d. On the 4th, the beach at Rota was examined, and was reported by the Engineers to be favourable for the disembarkation of the troops, and preparations were accordingly made for landing the Army on the following day, 5th of October. In the course of the 5th of October, however, a conference took place, at which the Admiral, the General, Sir R. Bickerton, Captains Elphinstone and Morris of the Navy, and Colonels John Abercromby and Anstruther, were present. The Admiral pointed out to Sir R. Bickerton and the two naval captains the position in which he proposed to station the Fleet during the time that the Army should remain on shore. The above-named naval officers gave it as their opinion that they considered the proposed anchorage to be unsafe at that season of the year. Lord Keith then, adopting the opinion of his officers, stated to the General that he could not insure him either a communication with the Fleet while the

Army was on shore, or a retreat to the ships in case a re-embarkation should become necessary.

Sir Ralph, although disappointed and staggered by the difficulties thus unexpectedly brought forward in the then advanced position of the enterprise, nevertheless desired to proceed, and during the discussions that ensued, he observed to the Admiral, that in most undertakings of the nature of that on which they were engaged, some hazards must be run; he stated that fourteen days would be required fully to carry out the spirit of his instructions, during which time communication with the Fleet was indispensable, but he offered to the Admiral, at the same time, to take the whole responsibility of the land service upon himself, and to share with him that which was attached to the Navy, adding, however, that if the Admiral would state it to be his opinion that the Army should not land, and that he could not insure uninterrupted communication with the Fleet for fourteen consecutive days, he would relinquish the project. Lord Keith wavered, and declined to say anything decisive. In this state of uncertainty, matters remained during the day of the 5th of October, but in the course of that evening Sir Ralph told the Admiral that before morning it would be necessary for him to come to a final determination. At two o'clock on the morning of the 6th of October, Sir Ralph left his bed, and went to the cot of Lord Keith, requesting to know from his Lordship what his decision on this important point was.

Lord Keith being either still undecided, or unwilling to give a direct opinion, Sir Ralph stated, that unless he would positively say to him that he ought not to land, he must desire that the troops should be disembarked in the morning, to which Lord Keith made no reply.

The order for the disembarkation of the troops on the 6th of October was however issued, but it was not till one o'clock in the afternoon of that day, that 3000 instead of 5000 men could be placed in the boats preparatory to landing. The ineffective arrangements made for the disembarkation and landing of the troops can be best explained by the following passages from a letter written by General Moore who commanded the Reserve, and who had been charged with the duty of conducting the landing:—

"Lord Keith was frightened at the opinion of his officers, and somewhat ashamed of what he had before asserted. He could not be got to adopt the opinion of his officers, nor totally to give up his own, though in my presence he was pushed by Sir Ralph to do so, who wished for a decided opinion from him, one way or another, that we might either immediately land, or return to Gibraltar.

"When the signal was made for landing, the Fleet was then under way, at least ten miles from the shore. The flat-bottomed boats, agreeably to the signal, began to assemble round the ships which contained the troops destined for that service. It is not to be described the bad arrangements and confusion which attended the assembling of the boats ; it was increased by the ships being under sail. About one o'clock P.M., there were only 3000 instead of 5000 men in boats, and no more boats could be got, and this from want of arrangement. We were seven miles from the shore, and before it would have been possible to land us and return for more troops, it must have been dark. It was evident, therefore, that the landing was to be effected with 3000 instead of 5000 men, and these, instead of being immediately supported by a second division of 5000 men, must trust to themselves for the night in an unknown country. Under these circumstances, Sir Ralph wisely determined to postpone the landing."

On Sir Ralph's return on board the "Foudroyant"

from the Phæton frigate in which he had been close in shore for the purpose of reconnoitring, and of being present in the event of the troops being able to land,[1] "Colonel Anstruther represented to him the necessity of having something in writing from Lord Keith, as he, Sir Ralph, was taking the whole responsibility on himself, and this became the more necessary, as it was obvious that all the naval officers were against the attempt, and as his Lordship himself had said after we had left his ship to land, that Sir Ralph was going to do a very rash act. In the evening of the 6th of October, Sir Ralph wrote to Lord Keith, stating that this was a conjoint expedition; and that, as by his instructions he was directed not to attack Cadiz, unless he saw a good prospect of being able to re-embark his army, he must require from him, as Commander-in-Chief of the Fleet, a positive answer whether or not he could promise him that; and, at the same time, he said, his Lordship's reply must decide his conduct. Lord Keith in his answer said, that at this season of the year, he could not promise him a safe retreat to his ships, or a communication while on shore; that, if he anchored his Fleet between Rota and Santa Catalina, in the event of a gale of wind, many of his ships

[1] Letter of Colonel John Abercromby, 12th October 1800.

must be lost; that, if he anchored farther out, and was, from stress of weather, obliged to put to sea, it might be weeks before he could return. He further said, that, as Sir Ralph had asked his opinion, he would advise him by no means to land, and concluded by saying that, if he did, he conceived that he would be acting contrary to the spirit of his instructions. Upon this Sir Ralph agreed not to persevere, as he could not venture to take so much responsibility on himself."

The circumstances which occurred previously to the enterprise being undertaken, and the course pursued by Lord Keith, are fully developed in the following minute dictated by Sir Ralph, of what had passed between himself and the Admiral:—

" His Majesty's Ministers having been pleased to order Sir Ralph Abercromby and Lord Keith to make a joint attack on the bay and city of Cadiz, it became the General's duty to weigh seriously in his mind the object in view, and the mode of accomplishing it. After carefully surveying Tofino's chart of the Bay of Cadiz, and after examining at Gibraltar those persons who were most likely to give information, it appeared to him that nothing could be effected by surprise or a *coup-de-main*, because the enemy could not have remained ignorant of our intention, and must necessarily have made such preparations as they had in their power to resist the impending attack. It appeared to him practicable to carry his orders into execution, provided a safe anchorage could be obtained for the Fleet, which would have enabled him when on shore to have kept up a communication with it, and to have re-embarked the troops in case of emergency. If his instructions had not positively enjoined him not to land the troops unless he was convinced in his own mind of the practicability of re-embarking them, he should equally have thought himself bound not to do it, because he always considered it as a fixed principle that no conjoint expedition of any magnitude should be undertaken unless the Fleet could be placed in a safe port. Reasoning on this principle, he thought that the anchorage from Rota to Santa Catalina would afford that security to the Fleet which was required, and would give to the Army those advantages which it was necessary they should possess. As the town of Rota is fortified towards the sea, and as there are several batteries between that place and Santa Catalina, which is a fort of considerable strength, it might have proved difficult for the ships of war to have silenced their batteries, and to have enabled the troops to land under them. To obviate these difficulties, it was found that there is a sandy beach to the northward of Rota where the troops might be landed; and it was proposed by the General, that as soon as they were disembarked they should make themselves masters of Rota, and the batteries between that and Santa Catalina. It was likewise intended (as soon as some pieces of artillery could be got on shore) to attack vigorously that fort. This plan was submitted to Lord Keith, and the principal pilot was examined on the sufficiency of the anchorage, who gave it as his opinion that in most winds it was safe. The Admiral, after examining the plan, acquiesced in the practicability of it, reserving, however, his final determination till such time as he should have seen Sir Richard Bickerton, who commanded the squadron cruising off Cadiz, and from whom he might receive information with which he was unacquainted. The General does not know that Sir R. Bickerton did communicate any intelligence of any moment which could particularly induce a change of opinion as to the anchorage in question. Sir R. Bickerton, and several other naval officers of character, seemed, however, to be of opinion that the anchorage between Rota and Santa Catalina was hazardous. Lord Keith hesitated a little. The General told him that he would take the whole responsibility of the land service upon himself, and that he would share with him, as a man of honour, in everything relative to the naval risk; at the same time he expressed a desire that his Lordship would declare his sentiments clearly on a subject of so much importance. Not having been able to obtain from his Lordship any explicit declaration, the General told his Lordship that he would take the whole responsibility upon himself, and that the landing must take place unless his Lordship should absolutely say that it should not. The orders were accordingly given, but from causes which the General is unable to explain, the troops did not get into the flat boats until late in the day, and even then not above one-half of the number ordered according to the arrangement which had been made with his Lordship. As the boats had more than four miles to row to the shore, it was evident that a sufficient number of troops could not be landed that evening, so as to have enabled them to maintain themselves on shore with any degree of security. This was apparent to the General and to Sir John Moore, who was to command the first body of troops that were to disembark; and they were therefore ordered to return to their respective ships. The General, who had been on board the 'Phæton' close in shore, did not observe any appearance which indicated a design on the part of the enemy to have seriously opposed the landing on that part of the coast, and he is fully persuaded, that if the frigates to cover the landing had been placed over night, and if the ships with the troops had gone early in the morning into nine-fathom water, that the whole, or the greater part of the troops, might have been disembarked in the course of that day. When the General returned from the 'Phæton' to the flag-ship, he found that the Admiral had expressed himself explicitly on the rashness of the undertaking, which led to a further conversation on the subject, and induced the General to ask his Lordship to express his opinion either affirmatively or negatively as to the possibility of re-embarking the troops in case of emergency. His Lordship then, in answer to this question, gave it as his opinion that he could not, and advised the General by no means to land the troops. The General did not, under these circumstances, think that he could disembark the troops and proceed in this operation, because his instructions did not permit him to land them unless he was convinced that they could be re-embarked with safety."

The expedition then returned to Gibraltar.

Sir Ralph was much distressed by the thought of the impression which could not fail to be made by this useless display of force at Cadiz, which would be aggravated by the previous failure at Ferrol; but he endeavoured to mitigate the disappointment which would be felt, and the censure which might be pronounced, by making the most of such reasons as could be urged to justify the abandonment of the enterprise.

Sir Henry Bunbury states, and apparently on good authority, that when at Gibraltar, Sir Ralph had received intelligence that the yellow fever, in its most fatal form, was raging in and about Cadiz. In consequence it had occurred to Sir Ralph, that it would be prudent to suspend operations against a town suffering under such a calamity, and he had proposed to the Admiral that they should repair to the Tagus, there to await fresh instructions from England. To this Lord Keith had decidedly objected, urging that the instructions were peremptory, especially as regarded the attack on the arsenals of the Caraccas, and Sir Ralph had acquiesced, though reluctantly, in the prosecution of the enterprise. The instructions were, probably, peremptory, but the question was, whether humanity might not have induced the Government to change their views, if they were made aware of the disastrous calamity under which Cadiz was suffering.

From the foregoing narrative of this expedition, it cannot be doubted that the conduct of the Admiral must have created embarrassments and difficulties for the General; and justice to Sir Ralph, and to the Army he commanded, would not have been done had it been passed over in silence.

CHAPTER VII.

EXPEDITION TO EGYPT.

1800-1801.

THE Fleet returned to Gibraltar, where it suffered much inconvenience from the prevalence of boisterous weather, and was dispersed, but happily no ships were lost.

The scurvy also broke out in several regiments, and rapidly extended, as the necessary means for arresting its progress could not be procured. This distressing position of the Fleet and of the Army was terminated by the arrival of the brig " Lavinia" on the 24th of October, with despatches for Sir Ralph and for Lord Keith.

These despatches informed Sir Ralph that the Government in England had decided upon sending an expedition to Egypt, with the view of expelling the French from that country, and they contained instructions directing him, if possible, to effect that object.

Such an expedition was in accordance with the views of Sir Ralph, as calculated to give security to important English interests, and to facilitate negotiations for peace.

At the close of the campaign in 1793, he had formed the opinion that a spirit was abroad which could not be put down by the force of arms, that, like the Reformation, it would not stop until it had travelled throughout Europe, and had either subverted or radically reformed the worn-out monarchies of the Continent. This opinion he communicated at the time to one of his Majesty's Ministers, and strongly advised that the first opportunity for making peace should be cordially and promptly seized. So long as the prosecution of the War was inevitable, he wished that it should be conducted by wisely directed efforts so that the spirit of the country and the honour of English arms should be sustained, as the sound means of securing peace, and, especially, that no favourable or legitimate opportunity to advance English interests should be lost, as the only compensation that could be obtained for the enormous expense incurred.

General Moore, on this occasion, writing from Malta on the 18th of December, says :— " The Army, I think, rather likes the service on which we are about to be employed; I, in particular, prefer it to anything that has yet offered. I am persuaded of the necessity of driving the French from Egypt before we can make peace. Sir Ralph is quite keen about it, and is ten years younger since he left England."

The ardour with which General Moore describes that Sir Ralph engaged in this service, which, from his advanced years, and from the progress of a painful complaint to which he was subject, would probably have been his last active employment, even if he had not fallen in the performance of it, can be easily understood by those who were familiar with his character.

Although in every service in which Sir Ralph had been engaged during the War, his conduct had been such as to have increased his reputation, and the confidence of the public and of the Army in his ability as a commander; he was disappointed and depressed by reflecting that with the exception of the conquest of French and Spanish islands in the West Indies, and the surrender of the Dutch fleet at the Helder, they had not been crowned with ultimate success nor rewarded by any solid advancement of English interests. He had suffered most acutely from the unfortunate conclusion of the expedition to Holland in 1793, and from the recent failure at Cadiz. With such feelings, it is not surprising that he embraced with ardour the opportunity now offered of engaging in an enterprise which gratified the honourable ambition by which all his exertions were animated, and enabled him to make a last effort to associate his name with a service which promised to be successful, to raise the character of the British Army, to strengthen the substantial interests of his country, and eventually to restore peace to Europe.

Before entering on the details of the military operations which finally led to the expulsion of the French from Egypt, it is just to Mr. Dundas, who was the sole author of the measure, to unfold the motives which influenced him in deciding to undertake that great and urgent enterprise.

The battle of Marengo, and the disastrous defeats sustained by the Austrian army, had rendered all hope of useful or efficient co-operation with them in Italy utterly desperate. The party in England who had so long and confidently cherished the hope that a counter-revolution might be effected in France by the exertions of French royalists, had at last become sensible that prudence would not sanction the encouragement and support of such visionary projects. The sagacity of Mr. Dundas enabled him to discern, and the manliness of his character led him to acknowledge the errors that had been committed in the conduct of the War. He saw that an enormous expenditure of money had been incurred, that a large military force had either been kept inactive or misdirected, and that much valuable time had been sacrificed. Under these circumstances, it appeared to Mr. Dundas, that it was his duty to his country to assert his opinion, as the Minister intrusted with the conduct of the War, and to make a vigorous effort to repair past errors, and to arrest the progress of the public disappointment and despondency produced by the uniformity of failure and defeat which had attended our Allies, and which had so strongly characterized the last campaign. Mr. Dundas was therefore anxious to revive the drooping spirits, and to retrieve the military character of the country, by directing our efforts to the attainment of objects calculated to promote English interests. He first turned his thoughts to the ports of Spain, and projected the expeditions to Ferrol and Cadiz. Foiled in these objects, he next directed his attention to the expulsion of the French from Egypt. Mr. Dundas having with great difficulty obtained the concurrence of the

King and of the Cabinet, it was finally decided, that the expedition to Egypt should be undertaken, and he immediately wrote to Sir Ralph a very full and unreserved detail of all that had passed in consequence of the proposal which had been made by France, to conclude a naval armistice, and of the counter proposition by England to negotiate in conjunction with Austria, for a general peace.

Mr. Dundas proceeded thus :—" Instead of entering into a general comparison between the advantages (if any still exist), of our sending a Minister to a Congress, or negotiating separately with France, I shall confine myself to giving you, as my opinion, that we ought to shun the former, and take the first opportunity of entering seriously upon the latter. Other persons may have different sentiments, but the necessary course of events, seems to counteract *their views,* as much as they accord with mine upon this momentous subject, which are, that a negotiation without a naval armistice, is the best line we can follow for bringing the War to a safe and not disgraceful conclusion, and Providence seems to interfere to prevent our adopting any other. Entertaining this opinion, I have no uneasiness with respect to the footing on which we shall meet the enemy, except what arises from his being in possession of

Egypt. From the moment of the unfortunate rupture of the Convention of El Arisch, I have watched with unceasing concern the unavailing efforts made by the Turks to drive him from that province, and coupling the weakness of that ally, with the disasters of our other Allies on the Continent, and the direction of British politics during this campaign, I own I have seen with great alarm the necessary moment of negotiation draw near, without perceiving any certainty that either by any military effort, pending that negotiation, or by any compensation it might afford us an opportunity of offering to the enemy, it would be in our power to compel or entice the French to withdraw from Egypt. My apprehension respecting the views or feelings of the present French Government upon this subject, were fully confirmed, both by the verbal and written discussions we had with Monsieur Otto, their agent here, respecting the armistice. The main difficulties of it have all turned upon the demand (still unrelinquished) of permission to send arms, military stores, and reinforcements to Egypt; and the explanations entered into by Monsieur Otto leave very little doubt, that a wish to establish their power in that country is the leading principle of their conduct in this instance, as it probably would be in any future negotiation. I enclose for your perusal, a paper which I lately circulated among his Majesty's Ministers, by which you will be made acquainted with my general opinions on this subject, and the little chance we have of frustrating the views of Bonaparte, unless adequate measures are immediately taken for this purpose. The idea I had formed when I wrote that paper of the difficulty to which we should be reduced, if nothing could be undertaken against Egypt, before or pending a negotiation is this: That we might go to the utmost possible extent of our offers of compensation from the conquests we have made; France would say in reply, If you think this is an equivalent for Egypt, we do not, and we cannot therefore agree to the exchange, as we are willing you should keep this equivalent, and we will keep Egypt. What answer can we make? We must either admit the reasoning, and subscribe to the premises, or break off the negotiation. In fact, we should have no choice, for we should not feel ourselves at liberty to adopt the other alternative. All that I have seen or heard confirms to me, that upon the question of Egypt, more or less modified, will turn the whole of our negotiation, and it is in order to take away from the enemy all the advantages they expect from it, or, if they cannot be taken away entirely, to divide, or (if I may use the expression) to neutralize them, that we now send you up the Mediterranean."

Mr. Dundas then proceeds to explain what he means by neutralizing the advantages which the enemy derive from the possession of Egypt. He says :—

"From the moment that we hear of your arrival at the proposed rendezvous (whether Rhodes, Cyprus, Candia, or the coast of Syria), we shall have a right, if then in negotiation with France, to consider ourselves as in a situation to dispute with them the possession of Egypt, even if the state of the weather and the season of the year should not admit of your making an immediate landing on the coast. If it should, or at any rate as soon as possible, you will proceed against Alexandria and the other ports, to endeavour to make yourself master of the whole extent of coast. My opinion is, that from the moment Alexandria falls, and the enemy find themselves pressed by the Turks on the side of Syria, you will be able to command the evacuation on granting moderate terms; but if I am mistaken in this expectation, still, by having the whole extent of coast in our hands, and by the measures taken to secure the ports on the Red Sea, we shall have a clear right to consider Egypt as at least a divided possession, for the evacuation of the interior of which France will be able to claim no other return than our retiring from the coast. By this arrangement, every other advantage of the negotiation, as far as relates to sacrifices and restitutions, will be on our side, and upon this one point, instead of it being in their power to set it off against or to hold it higher than any other, we shall be upon a footing of equality, which is the least benefit we have reason to expect from the expedition on which you are now to proceed."

These sound and enlightened views of Mr. Dundas afford full evidence of the earnestness with which he laboured to conclude a separate peace, on safe and not dishonourable terms, and his conviction that the attainment of this great object depended entirely on the success of the expedition to Egypt. His able and convincing reasoning encountered much opposition from his colleagues, and, on a separate ground, from the King. In writing to Sir Ralph, Mr. Dundas said :—" The deep impression I have of the French being disappointed in their views upon Egypt, has made me uncommonly urgent in pressing these opinions on his Majesty's confidential servants. Indeed, it would be unfair and uncandid in me not to acknowledge that if the country meets with any serious disappointment in the event or consequences of this enterprise, the responsibility does and ought to rest upon me, as many doubts and objections have been stated against it by persons of great respectability."

The objection of the King was founded on an opinion which had been infused into his mind, that the climate of Egypt would prove more fatal to the troops than the yellow fever had ever been in the most unhealthy of the West India islands. It is a proper tribute to the candour of the King, to state that after the accounts of the first successes in Egypt had been received, he took an occasion to state, in the presence of many persons, his respect for the Minister who had the courage and the virtue to persevere in the promotion of this great enterprise, in opposition to his opinion, and to that of many members of the Government.

Having shown how courageously Mr. Dundas had assumed the whole responsibility of suggesting and of planning the enterprise, and how deeply his character and fame as a Minister were involved in the result, it only remains to point out with what confidence he relied on the commander to whom the conduct of the expedition had been intrusted.

After putting Sir Ralph in possession of the facts on which his own opinion had been formed, Mr. Dundas says, " I do not mean to exclude your further inquiry, or even an exercise of your judgment, if the result of further inquiry should lead you to form a decided opinion contrary to the instructions you have received. From the naval advice you have with you, and the various channels of information which the Mediterranean affords, it is not impossible you may receive such information and intelligence, either with respect to the navigation to Egypt, or with regard to the circumstances in which that country now is, as may induce you either in whole or in part to postpone the execution of the service committed to your charge, and I shall not repine at whatever the exercise of that discretion may be. In your hands I feel the interests of the country safe in this respect. I do not mean these as common expressions of complimentary address, because I know that as on the one hand no false point of honour or feeling will induce you to attempt what is too hazardous to be attempted, so, on the other hand, I am satisfied by experience, that when great objects are at stake, and great services are in contemplation, you are not to be startled by those difficulties to which characters of less energy or less standing than your own may allow themselves to yield."

The clear and candid revelation of his views contained in the letters of Mr. Dundas, from which only partial extracts can with propriety be given, must have been very acceptable to Sir Ralph, as indicating a striking coincidence of opinion as to the desirableness of concluding a separate peace, and as to the objects to which the disposable force of England ought in the meanwhile to be directed.

The expulsion of the French from Egypt, and the emancipation of South America, were two objects to which Sir Ralph had drawn the attention of the Government in a Memorial,[1] which he had at a former time submitted for their consideration. However he might have wished that a preference had been given at an earlier period to the latter object, he now felt that the turn of affairs on the Continent, the prospect of an early negotiation for peace, and the circumstances in which the disposable force of the country was then placed, all combined to decide the question in favour of an effort to expel the French from Egypt. This opinion was expressed in a letter to Mr. Huskisson, then Under-Secretary to Mr. Dundas, and of whose abilities Sir Ralph entertained a very

[1] *Vide* Appendix A.

high opinion, in which he says, " I ardently wish that public affairs may go well, and they cannot go better than in obtaining, what I have always longed for, a reasonable peace. I think you are now beginning to be sensible. I wish you had laid aside your buckram opinions a little sooner."

This letter to Mr. Huskisson was written before Sir Ralph was aware that the expedition to Egypt had been finally decided on; and its contents must have assured Mr. Dundas, that his opinions and instructions on the subject would be favourably and cordially received by the General he had appointed to command the enterprise. Sir Ralph, on his part, must have felt that the confidence thus placed in him, and the discretion with which he was invested, carried with them a responsibility which required that all the energies of his mind should be devoted to the undertaking in which he was about to engage. The watchful care, the zeal, and the undaunted resolution with which he exercised his discretionary powers under circumstances often embarrassing and discouraging, will be seen by tracing the outline of the military operations from their commencement to the close of the decisive battle on the 21st March 1801.

Immediately after the arrival at Gibraltar of the

brig "Lavinia," on the 24th October 1800, with despatches for Sir Ralph, an order was issued, announcing that a separation of the Army was to take place. Major-Generals Hutchinson, Coote, Cradock, Ludlow, Moore, Lord Cavan, and Brigadier-Generals Stuart, Hope, Doyle, and Oakes, were attached to the division of the Army destined to serve under Sir Ralph. Brigadier-General Hope and Colonel Anstruther were appointed Adjutant and Quartermaster-Generals. The total effective strength of the regiments of infantry amounted to 13,488. The total of cavalry was only 200. The artillery, under Brigadier-General Lawson, amounted to 614 men; and the engineers, under Major M'Kerras, consisted only of a few artificers. The selection of general officers chosen for this service was, on the whole, judicious and satisfactory; and the infantry regiments were, with the exception of three battalions lately completed from the Irish militia, old soldiers who had not been much employed on home service, were in good order, and for the most part well commanded. The composition of this Army was equal, or perhaps superior, to any that had been assembled by England during the war. It was impossible to conceal the destination of the armament. It was necessarily known that the troops were to be employed in the Mediterranean; and as no regiments were selected but those in which the men had been enlisted for general service, the conclusion was obvious that Egypt must be the object of the enterprise.

The original intention was that all the fleet should touch at Minorca, and with that view the first division, consisting of about twenty ships, sailed on the 27th of October for that island. At the same time Colonel Anstruther, the Quartermaster-General, and Lieutenant-Colonel Murray, sailed for Rhodes with instructions to communicate with the Turkish army in Syria, and to make all necessary preparations to facilitate the future progress of the enterprise.

In order to avoid delay, it was subsequently decided that only such ships should touch at Minorca as required repairs that could not be made at Malta, to which place all the rest of the fleet were to proceed direct.

It is to be regretted that there were causes which diminished the effective strength of the Army, even before it left Gibraltar. The troop-ships, with very rare exceptions, were in a most wretched condition, deficient in anchors and stores of every kind; the decks so leaky that when it rained the men were constantly wet; they were too much crowded, and the soldiers, with no other bedding than blankets, were obliged to lie on the deck. The sick, amounting to between four and five hundred, were left in the general hospital at Gibraltar; and the second battalion of the 27th Regiment of Infantry, in which a bad fever had broken out, were in consequence sent to Lisbon in the ships in which they had been embarked to sail up the Mediterranean.

On the 5th of November 1800 all the ships in Gibraltar Bay, belonging to the expedition, got under way and sailed for Tetuan. After a quick passage, Sir Ralph, who sailed in the "Diadem" of 74 guns, reached Malta in the afternoon of the 19th of November. The weather had been boisterous, and the ships had been dispersed, so that some time elapsed before the whole fleet re-assembled. As circumstances rendered some delay at Malta indispensable, Sir Ralph landed on the 20th, and he anxiously wished that, if possible, the troops should be disembarked; but this most desirable object could not be effected, in consequence of the impossibility of finding quarters for them. Every precaution was adopted to remedy this inconvenience. The men of some of the regiments that were most sickly were accommodated in tolerable barracks in the town and in the adjoining villages. The troops were directed to be landed as frequently as possible for the benefit of exercise, and to give time for cleaning the ships thoroughly; they were invariably supplied with fresh beef, and with an abundance of vegetables.

Sir Ralph had, while at Minorca, made a tour of that island, and examined carefully the means of defence, the advantages which it offered, and all other circumstances which could affect its value in the event of its becoming a possession of Great Britain. At Malta he followed the same course, and knowing from his instructions that an early negotiation for peace was probable, he transmitted to Mr. Dundas, before proceeding on the expedition, the opinion which he had formed of the comparative value of Minorca and Malta, and also of the preliminary steps which ought to be taken, with a view to the establishment of a regular government, in the event of Malta (to which he gave the preference) becoming a permanent possession of England.[1]

The information which the Government had collected for the guidance of Sir Ralph, in the conduct of the expedition, was most meagre. In fact, it

[1] *Vide* Appendix B

consisted only of a very bad map of Egypt, and of copies of a work which had been published under the title of " Intercepted Correspondence," on which no reliance could safely be placed. Sir Ralph was therefore anxiously engaged while at Malta in endeavouring to obtain information respecting the strength, state, and condition of the French army in Egypt, the geography of the country, and the nature of the works recently constructed for the defence of Alexandria. Except with respect to the weather which generally prevails on the coast of Egypt, and to the facilities for disembarkation afforded by the Bay of Aboukir, the information was most contradictory and unsatisfactory.

The impression left on Sir Ralph's mind may be estimated by the following extract from a letter which he wrote to Mr. Dundas before leaving Malta : " During my stay here, I have procured a little information respecting Egypt, and have been able to form some notion on the operations of the campaign, with which I shall not trouble you at present, but I think it necessary to apprise you that the service on which we are going will not probably be so soon performed as you may expect."

It was the wish and intention of the Government that the expedition should have sailed direct from

Malta to Egypt. It was, however, necessary to proceed to a third rendezvous, for the purpose of taking in a full supply of water, receiving a great quantity of small craft, horses, and refreshments for the troops, and also to leave the sick. All necessary arrangements having been completed, the Fleet was ready to have sailed from Malta on the 13th of December 1800, but the wind being adverse, it was not until the morning of the 20th that the first division of the Fleet was enabled to weigh anchor. On the morning of the 27th, the "Kent," in which Sir Ralph sailed, and the first division of the Fleet, being off Rhodes, they fell in with the "Peterel," sloop, which Sir Sidney Smith had left to conduct them into the Bay of Marmorice, where they anchored in the afternoon. On the 2d January 1801, the second division of the Fleet arrived in Marmorice Bay.[1] The interval between the arrival of the Army at Marmorice, and the final departure for Egypt on the 22d of February, was employed by Sir Ralph in watchful and zealous attention to the health and discipline of the troops. The experience of the defective arrangements that had been made when a landing at Cadiz was attempted, showed the necessity for guarding against the recurrence of

[1] *Vide* Appendix C.

similar evils. The troops were constantly practised in embarking and disembarking, until both services became expert in the performance of that duty.

As the expulsion of the French from Egypt, and the restitution of that province to the Porte, was the ultimate object of the expedition, it was reasonable to expect the most zealous and cordial support from the Turkish Government. To ascertain how far reliance could be placed on this expected co-operation, was one of the first subjects that engaged the attention of Sir Ralph. Before the fleet sailed from Gibraltar, Colonel Anstruther, Quartermaster-General, was sent to Rhodes to make the necessary arrangements for the contemplated service, and Lieutenant-Colonel Murray was directed to proceed to the camp of the Grand Vizir at Jaffa. The first reports received from Colonel Anstruther were very encouraging, but unhappily they were founded on warm professions of friendship, and promises of cordial assistance and co-operation which proved eventually to be quite illusory. Lieutenant-Colonel Murray had arrived from the camp of the Vizir before Sir Ralph reached Marmorice, and his report of the Turkish Army was so discouraging as to preclude all hope of useful or efficient co-operation. Sir Ralph still deemed it advisable to send an officer of rank to announce to the Grand Vizir the arrival of the English force at Marmorice, to explain the operations that might be undertaken, and to encourage him to put his army in a condition fit for active service. General Moore was selected for that mission, and his report entirely confirmed that which had been previously made by Lieutenant-Colonel Murray, and, he added, that it was his decided opinion that the plan of operations ought not in any degree to be influenced by the hope of assistance from the Turks, which could not at present be expected.

This report did not make any alteration in Sir Ralph's views, for very soon after his arrival at Marmorice, he had become convinced that the Turks regarded the armament with a jealous eye, and did nothing to assist, and much to thwart and obstruct the preparations for the enterprise. This system was so constantly pursued by the Turks, that the Fleet finally sailed from Marmorice without any official authority from them to countenance the expedition, and unaccompanied by a single Turkish soldier or ship. It may be that the Turks were alarmed at the magnitude of the armament, and may have suspected that the expulsion of the French was not the only object in view. All possible pains were used, but without apparent success, to remove this suspicion. It may be that the Emperor Paul, who was then on the eve of declaring war against England, and of forming an alliance with France, may have been induced by the French Government to threaten an immediate invasion of the Turkish dominions, unless all assistance to the English expedition were withheld, and the Turks may have preferred the sacrifice of Egypt to the danger of an incursion which they may have felt that they were unable to resist.

Whatever the motive may have been which influenced the conduct of the Turkish Government at that time, it added greatly to the difficulties of the Commander, and left him no resource but in his own energy, and in the bravery of his troops. It was now placed beyond all doubt that no present assistance would be afforded by the Turks, and that future co-operation could only be expected in the event of such a footing being gained by the Army in Egypt as would justify a reasonable hope of ultimate success. In that case it was probable that both the inhabitants of the country, and the Turkish Government, would be disposed to assist in the expulsion of the French. Under these circumstances it became necessary to weigh carefully the scanty and inconclusive information which had been collected, and to decide upon a plan of operations commensurate with the means and strength of the English Army, which was now to act independently and unsupported by the Turks. The instructions given to Sir Ralph simply suggested the expediency of landing at the nearest practicable point to Alexandria, but he was authorized to exercise his own discretion, and to substitute any other plan which he might deem more advisable.

The gravity and responsibility of the decision then to be made, must not be judged by the events which followed, but must be tested by reference to the imperfect information which had been with difficulty and exertion obtained, and in the accuracy of which, on material points, no confident reliance could be placed. The anchorage in the Bay of Aboukir was known to be good, and it was believed that constant communication with the Fleet could be maintained, so that, if circumstances should render re-embarkation necessary, it could most probably be effected with little loss. Aboukir, on these grounds, offered advantages as the place of disembarkation ; but, as the disposition and amount of the French force were entirely unknown, it was not impossible that the enemy, suspecting or knowing that we should land there, might have assembled such a force as would have rendered the attempt impracticable. This was the more to be apprehended, as there was every reason to believe that the ground between the Castle of Aboukir and Lake Maadieh did not exceed a league. The landing being successfully effected, the next object would necessarily be to obtain possession of Alexandria, by which a safe harbour would be secured for the Fleet, and a position for the Army, from which arrangements might be made for moving against the enemy wherever their force might be concentrated, and which, even under adverse circumstances, might be maintained, until reinforcements could be received. It was believed that the French had so strengthened Alexandria, that it could not be taken by a *coup-de-main*, and, therefore, that the use of artillery must be the resource. There were neither horses nor mules to draw the artillery, and no prospect of obtaining a sufficient number of either for that purpose, so that this laborious service must be devolved on the troops. Mr. Baldwin, who had been nearly thirty years consul at Cairo and at Alexandria, who being at Naples when the Fleet was at Malta, had handsomely volunteered his services, and now accompanied the expedition, gave it as his decided opinion, that no fresh water would be found on the peninsula between Aboukir and Alexandria.

This opinion of Mr. Baldwin was confirmed not only by travellers, but by every individual who had been examined on this point.

All authorities concurred in stating that the coast between Aboukir and Alexandria was so rocky, and the surf so high, that no boats could approach the shore, except in one small creek about four miles from Alexandria, and then only in favourable weather. The direction of Lake Maadieh could not be determined with certainty, but Mr. Baldwin and others who were examined, agreed in stating that the nearest portion of it was distant four or five miles from Alexandria. It did not, therefore, appear that much assistance could be derived from the lake in conducting operations against Alexandria, and it was probable that it might become necessary to trust to the Fleet to supply the Army with water, wood, provisions, and stores of every kind. This supply must, in bad weather, have been drawn from Aboukir, a distance of ten miles, or, in favourable weather, from the Creek, a distance of five miles by land, and five miles by water, as all the ships must have permanently remained at Aboukir. This was a demand on the Navy, which even the greatest activity and energy on their part might have been unequal to meet. The French, after throwing a sufficient garrison into Alexandria, might have a disposable force, capable of obstructing the operations of a siege, and the strong body of cavalry which they were known to possess would materially assist in impeding the progress of the service.

In addition to these anticipated difficulties, the progress of the equipment at Marmorice was retarded by events which were not under the control of the Commander, and the means of the Army were crippled by the failure of arrangements which the Government at home had directed to be made at Constantinople and at Smyrna. Horse-ships and small craft which had been taken up at Smyrna two months previously, did not, from some unexplained mismanagement, arrive at Marmorice until the 17th of February, although the distance is only two days' sail.

Five hundred mules had been purchased at Smyrna, and the "Greyhound" frigate, which had long before been sent to convoy them, joined the Fleet after it had sailed from Marmorice, with the intelligence that the vessels in which the mules had been embarked had been dispersed in a gale, and had taken refuge in different ports. The horses which Lord Elgin[1] had been directed to purchase at Constantinople, only arrived on the 17th of February, and were found to be in such miserable condition, that very few of them were fit for the purpose for which they had been intended.

In a letter from Sir Ralph to Colonel Brownrigg, from Marmorice Bay, dated 16th February 1801, he thus describes his view of the prospects of the expedition :—

"It is impossible for me to say how much we have been disappointed in our expectations of assistance from the Turkish Government. I firmly believe, that both the Quartermaster-General and Lord Elgin did use, before our arrival here, every exertion to procure us those articles of which we stood most in need, and I know, from my own experience, the impossibility of rousing the Turks to any effectual aid or co-operation. We are now on the point of sailing for the coast of Egypt, with very slender means for executing the orders we have received. I never went on any service entertaining greater doubts of success, at the same time with more determination to encounter difficulties. Our own character, and the honour of the profession to which we belong, urge us all to use every effort in

[1] Then British Ambassador at Constantinople.

the discharge of our duty. The Dutch expedition was walking on velvet in comparison with this. Do not think that this is a gloomy letter, I only wish that you should know the truth."

In a letter to Mr. Huskisson of the same date, and on the same subject, Sir Ralph thus expresses himself:—

"The Turkish Government has been lavish of promises, but in no one circumstance have they been fulfilled, and we now go to fight their battles without their assistance or co-operation in any one article. I am not willing to state difficulties, but I should deceive you if I did not speak truth. You may rest assured that everything shall be done that it is possible to accomplish, but I cannot, and will not, promise success."

Before sailing from Gibraltar, the difficulty of finding specie in the Mediterranean had been urgently pressed on the consideration of the Government. Unhappily the admonition was not attended to, and the consequence was, that the pay of the troops was three months in arrear, and the military chest was nearly exhausted. One hundred horses for the cavalry had been purchased at Marmorice with the aid of the dollars which were contributed by the staff-officers out of their own resources.

It was calculated that eight or ten Turkish gunboats, which had been procured at Rhodes, together with two or three English gunboats which had been fitted up, would, with the assistance of the brigs and cutters, be found sufficient to cover the landing. The engineers had been employed in making facines and gabions, as Egypt furnishes no wood for such purposes, and every exertion was made to provide the Army with all that was necessary for the arduous service on which they were about to be employed. A few days before leaving Marmorice, a French corvette was brought in, which had been taken by one of Lord Keith's cruisers. This corvette had sailed from Toulon in company with two French frigates, which had succeeded in getting into Alexandria with 800 soldiers and military stores. It appeared from the contents of letters which were found on board the corvette, that there were several other frigates ready to sail from Toulon, and that it was the determination of Bonaparte to make every possible exertion, and at every hazard, to send supplies and reinforcements to Egypt.

Such were the difficulties to be overcome in the event of a landing being effected at Aboukir, and such were the means that had been provided for the conduct of the enterprise. It had been considered whether it would not be preferable to land at Damietta, and thence to proceed to Cairo, which the French had made their Capital. When the details of that operation were examined, however, so many serious objections to it presented themselves, that the Damietta plan was rejected, and the preference was given to Aboukir.

Although the armament had been some weeks at Marmorice, and every effort had been made to forward the equipment of the Army, the result had not corresponded with the exertions or expectations of the Commander.

The time for action had arrived, and a decision was to be formed under difficult and anxious circumstances.

Mr. Dundas had stated in his instructions that, when the armament had reached the place of rendezvous in the Mediterranean, he should consider that on our side the negotiators for peace would, from that moment, be entitled to maintain that the possession of Egypt was in dispute, and dependent on the result of an undecided contest, and their argument would be powerfully strengthened if a footing could be made in Egypt. If, on the other hand, the French, conjecturing that a landing would be attempted at Aboukir, should have assembled such a force as would, with the advantages of ground and position, have rendered the disembarkation impracticable; or if, after having effected a landing, the deficiency of our means, or the superiority of the enemy in number or resources, should make retreat necessary, then the whole object of the expedition would be at once and irretrievably defeated, and all the advantages in a negotiation for peace would be thrown into the scale of France.

On mature reflection, Sir Ralph determined, if possible, to effect a landing at Aboukir, and to follow it up as far as prudence and the means at his command would allow.

Having made up his mind, he announced his resolution to the general officers, and proceeded to carry it into effect; and from that moment to the hour of his death he proceeded with unfaltering and dauntless energy, tempered only by that caution which was imposed on him in acting on unknown ground, in conflict with an enemy with the amount of whose force he was unacquainted, and who commanded the resources of the country. The responsibility of the decision was increased by the instructions from England, which thus disclosed the material influence which the expedition might have, not only by its ultimate success, but by being protracted so long as negotiations for peace were pending.

Although the equipment of the Army was less satisfactory and complete than had been expected, yet, as the enemy were no doubt daily profiting from delay, Sir Ralph decided that the time had come when it was necessary to leave the Bay of Marmorice. Accordingly, orders were issued for the embarkation of the troops, and of the few horses which had been purchased. The order in which the troops were to disembark, and an excellent code of instructions for the conduct of the Army during the campaign, were also issued. All the ships were directed to have as large a supply of wood and water as they could possibly carry, and several ships were besides specially allotted for that purpose. The sick unfit for service were sent to an hospital which had been provided at Rhodes. The general officers were furnished with the best maps of Egypt that could be procured, and their instructions were full and distinct. The nature of the difficulties that were to be encountered were fully explained. The importance and necessity of maintaining the strictest discipline, and of paying the greatest attention to precision and regularity in the movement of the troops, were strongly impressed by the Commander, who concluded by assuring them that if they were so fortunate as to find water, there was every reason to flatter themselves with the hope of at least partial success.

The exact amount of the effective infantry was 14,144; but from that was to be deducted 750, who were not expected to be able to land with their regiments. The total of cavalry was 1063 men, and 454 horses. There were 630 artillerymen, with 173 horses. Lord Keith promised the aid of a Battalion of Marines consisting of 500 men, making a total of 16,337 men, and 627 horses.

These arrangements having been completed, the signal for the Fleet to sail was made at seven in the morning of the 22d February 1801, and before dusk the whole were clear of the harbour. Colonel Abercromby, in his journal, says :—" It was impossible not to contemplate with an awful but interesting sensation the noble sight of this grand fleet issuing from under the stupendous mountains of Asia Minor. Never was there an expedition attended with more important and extraordinary circumstances. Never was the honour of the British Army more at stake, or its animated exertions more required : and never was the interest of the country more deeply involved than in its ultimate success. Our difficulties, as far as we are now enabled to view them, are great indeed; but I can venture to assert that an equal number of Britons were never assembled who were more determined to uphold their own and their country's honour."

The weather proved to be variable and hazy, and on the 27th, the Fleet was dispersed by a very fresh gale, but re-assembled on the 28th, with the exception of some ships that were missing. On the 1st of March, the look-out frigates made the signal of seeing land, and the Fleet was ordered to bring-to. In the course of the evening, Captain Louis of the "Minotaur," who had been cruising off the coast, came on board the "Kent" to inform Sir Ralph that Major M'Kerras, the chief engineer, and Captain Fletcher of the same corps, who had been despatched from Marmorice to reconnoitre the coast, had unfortunately been surprised in a small boat, and had been made prisoners. A more untoward accident could not have occurred, as the services of the Chief Engineer were lost, and from the fact of his having been found in the Bay of Aboukir, the enemy could no longer be in doubt as to the place where the landing would be attempted. On the 3d of March, a flag of truce from Alexandria brought intelligence that Major M'Kerras had been killed by an accidental shot, the boat in which he was having made some resistance, the enemy had found it necessary to fire.

On the 2d of March, the greater part of the Fleet anchored in Aboukir Bay, and the signal to prepare to land was made, but the roughness of the sea, and the violence of the surf, rendered it impossible to do so. Sir Ralph, however, went close in shore, in a small vessel to reconnoitre, and the place of landing was chosen and fixed.

The north-west winds continuing to blow with unabated fury, the immediate landing of the troops was impracticable. On the 6th of March, Sir Sidney Smith was sent to destroy a gun-boat stationed at the entrance of Lake Maadieh, and to cut the rope which formed a pontoon bridge, by means of which the communication between Rosetta and Aboukir was kept up. A prisoner who was taken, gave information that 2000 men had been sent from Alexandria, together with a small body of cavalry and fifteen pieces of artillery, under General Friant, to oppose the landing. He also stated that a French frigate from Rochefort, with several hundred soldiers on board, had arrived at Alexandria the day after the English Fleet anchored in Aboukir Bay. This would not have happened if the cruisers off Alexandria had not unfortunately been recalled by Lord Keith.

At length the wind became moderate, and on the 8th of March the preparations for landing commenced. All the orders for the disembarkation of the Army had been made public before the departure from Marmorice. It was so arranged that each vessel knew to which particular ship the boats were to proceed on the signal being made for the First Division to prepare to land. In order to guard as far as possible against the chance of any mistake being made, the First Division was repeatedly landed in its regular order before leaving Marmorice. Two field-pieces, with the artillerymen attached to them, were put on board each of the line-of-battle ships, and the launches were so fitted up, that they could receive the guns, mounted on their carriages, by which means they would be landed, and ready to fire, nearly at the moment that the troops got on shore.

At two in the morning, on the 8th of March, a rocket was fired from Lord Keith's ship, which was the signal for preparing to land, and by three o'clock the troops of the first division began to get into the boats. Owing to the distance at which the ships lay from the shore, it was near eight o'clock before they reached the small vessels stationed to cover the landing, and round which they were directed to assemble. The troops were alive to the difficulty and danger of the service in which they were engaged, and, while they rowed to the rendezvous, the most profound silence was preserved, and not a sound was heard save the splashing of the oars in the sea. About fifty men sat in each of the boats with their muskets unloaded, and there were in all about 5000. On reaching the rendezvous, a little time was required to arrange the boats in their proper order. At nine o'clock, Captain Cochrane of the Navy, who superintended the arrangements for landing with great judgment and ability, made the signal to pull to shore. The troops, fixed to their seats, without the power of resistance or defence, exposed to the fire of fifteen pieces of artillery, throwing round grape shot, and shells, and to the musketry of 2000 infantry, remained undismayed, answering only with hurrahs, in anticipation of the victory which they so gloriously achieved. It has seldom, or perhaps never before happened, that a more concentrated fire was brought to bear upon a single and defenceless point. When the troops reached the shore, they had to contend with a force which was most advantageously posted.

The enemy had Lake Maadieh on their right, and a long commanding sand-hill on their left. The sand-hill had a very steep front towards the sea, and came down close to the edge of the water. The intermediate ground between this sand-hill and the right of the enemy was covered with a number of small and irregular sand-hills, on which artillery were placed, and behind them were the infantry and cavalry. The whole extent of ground between Lake Maadieh and the sea did not exceed a mile and half, and was entirely occupied by the enemy, except that portion of it which was within the range of the fire from the castle of Aboukir. General Moore, with the flank companies of the 40th, 23d, and 28th regiments, landed under the sand-hill, which was nearly perpendicular, and the troops sunk up to the knees in loose sand. General Moore, in a spirited and masterly manner, gained the sand-hill, thus turning the left of the enemy, who retired across a plain keeping up a distant and not well directed fire from their artillery. General Moore stopped the pursuit, as he heard a heavy firing on his left, which he knew must proceed from the remainder of the reserve which General Oakes was bringing up.

The 42d and 58th regiments, under General

Oakes, the brigade of Guards under General Ludlow, and a part of General Coote's brigade, landed opposite to the enemy's right and centre, where the resistance was very obstinate. On that point the contest was maintained for an hour, but the enemy, after the most strenuous efforts of their infantry, cavalry, and artillery, were forced to retire, leaving seven field-pieces, some ammunition-waggons, a few horses, and many of their wounded.

The plan of putting two field-pieces into the launches of the line-of-battle ships fully answered the expectations which had been formed, for they were landed and in action as soon as the troops. The enemy behaved with great courage; they sustained a severe loss of men, and General Martinet was killed. Nothing could resist the intrepidity of the English troops, which, as Sir Ralph expressed in his public despatch, could scarcely be paralleled. The apprehension that the French might have assembled a sufficient force to prevent the landing was removed, and a footing in Egypt had been gained. Before General Moore landed, Sir Ralph, who was in the nearest bomb-vessel, sent General Hope to say, "that if he (Sir Ralph) saw that the fire from the enemy was so great that the men could not bear it, he would make the signal to retire, and desired that he and Captain Cochrane should look occasionally to the ship in which he was;" thus evincing that humanity and feeling for the troops were the only limits to the exertions which he was prepared to make. From the vessel in which Sir Ralph was he had a full view of the preparations made by the enemy, and, after surveying them, he turned to General Hope and smiling, said, This is really taking the bull by the horns. General Hope, Colonel Abercromby, and some of those who were nearest to Sir Ralph, were well aware how difficult it would be to restrain him from landing with the first of the troops, and therefore they arranged with Lieutenant Richardson, who was to command the boat from which Sir Ralph was to land, that he should not push off from the bomb-vessel until he saw that the landing was securely effected. General Hope left the vessel in which Sir Ralph was, unobserved, as he believed, but he had scarcely gone before Sir Ralph called for his boat and was immediately put on shore, accompanied by his son Colonel Abercromby, and by Colonel Kempt, his military secretary, in full time to direct and to enjoy the conduct of the troops.[1]

---

[1] When Sir Ralph was at Malta, he inspected the 23d regiment, Welsh Fusileers, which had formerly served under him with distinction, and he was mortified to find that the corps was in the worst order and condition. A

Sir Ralph passed the night of the 8th of March, which was very cold, under a small hut formed from branches of the date-tree, which was constructed for him by the soldiers, who vied with each other in their efforts to mark their gratitude by providing shelter for a Commander who was the ever-watchful guardian of their health and comfort; a trifling incident, in itself unimportant, but which, being authentic, is strongly illustrative of the estimation in which the character of Sir Ralph as a Commander was held by those who served under him.

He was a just and severe disciplinarian, but prompt and frank in his approval of those who profited from his instruction.

On the 9th of March, the reserve advanced about two miles, and took up a position at Mandora, which is the narrowest part of the peninsula, the distance between the lake and the sea scarcely exceeding a mile. On this and the following day water of a tolerably good quality was found, thus disproving the testimony which had been given without a dissenting voice on this most important

general order was published strongly censuring the inefficiency of the regiment, and Brigadier-General Oakes was directed to assume, in person, the command of the regiment until he should be enabled to report that it was restored to efficiency. Soon after landing at Aboukir, Sir Ralph, having witnessed the gallantry of the flank companies of the 23d on the assault of the sand-hills, saw Lieutenant-Colonel Hall, who had resumed the command of that regiment, and going up to him, shook him cordially by the hand and said,— "My friend Hall, I am glad to see you; I shall never abuse you again."

point. On the 11th of March, some Arabs came in. This was a fortunate circumstance. In the instructions issued by Sir Ralph at Marmorice for the guidance of the officers and men under the various circumstances that might arise, "the utmost forbearance, and the most humane treatment of the inhabitants, the most scrupulous and honourable conduct in all their dealings, prompt payment for all supplies purchased, the greatest deference for their habits and religious tenets," were enjoined in forcible terms. The Arabs were encouraged to bring in supplies, and they were so well satisfied with their treatment, that within a few days after the Army had landed on the sandy and barren shore of Egypt, a market, under the direction of Mr. Baldwin, was established, which was well supplied by the inhabitants, in despite of an order issued by the French, annexing the penalty of death to those who were detected in conveying provisions to the camp of the invaders. So faithfully and exactly were Sir Ralph's orders observed, that from the day of his landing to the hour of his death he was never called upon to take cognizance of a single case of outrage or even ordinary misconduct on the part of either officer or soldier.

Provisions, stores, and other requisites having been landed by the unremitting exertions of the

Navy, the Army advanced five miles on the 12th of March, having been retarded and harassed by the Tirailleurs, and a considerable body of French cavalry, who were favoured by the ground, which was much broken by sand-hills, and woods of date-trees. Before our troops reached the ground on which it was intended to halt, a large body of the enemy's infantry was observed on an eminence, which extended nearly across the peninsula, and it appeared from their manœuvres as if they intended to descend to make an attack. A line was instantly formed, and the Army advanced in the best possible order for nearly half a mile, and halted on gaining a favourable piece of ground. The two armies were now separated by a plain not exceeding two miles in extent, and the enemy were posted on an advantageous ridge with the right to the canal of Alexandria, and the left towards the sea. The enemy showed no inclination to quit his favourable position, and the day being too far advanced to begin an attack, the troops were ordered to pile their arms, and to lie by them during the night. The position of the enemy having been reconnoitred, Sir Ralph determined to make an attack on the following morning, with a view to turn their right flank. Accordingly, the Army marched on the morning of the 13th of March in two columns, Major-General Cradock having the right, and Major-General Lord Cavan the left. The 90th regiment formed the advanced guard of the former, and the 92d regiment that of the latter. The artillery, though, from the want of horses to transport it, rather an encumbrance than an assistance, was disposed of to the best advantage in different parts of the line. Soon after our Army began to move, the enemy quitted his position, and commenced the attack. The brigade of Major-General Cradock was the first against which the enemy directed his efforts. The French cavalry made a bold and spirited attack on the 90th regiment, who, unbroken and undismayed, received them on the points of their bayonets. The cavalry retreated, and many of them fell under an effective volley of musketry, which was poured upon them as they wheeled. The brigade of Lord Cavan was nearly at the same time very sharply engaged, and the troops were ordered to deploy, which was effected with the greatest quickness and precision. After a warm contest, in which the fire on both sides was uncommonly severe, the French retreated in every direction in tolerable order, under the protection of their artillery, which was remarkably well served, and was very galling. The enemy did not halt on the position which he had occupied in the morning, but retreated across a plain of a mile in extent, and retired to a strong ridge of sand-hills which appeared to be within the range of fire from Alexandria. It was the intention of Sir Ralph to have followed up his success by attacking the last position taken up by the enemy, and driving them within the walls of Alexandria, and he had made the necessary arrangements for carrying his purpose into execution.

It had been decided that General Hutchinson should attack the right, and that the reserve, under General Moore, supported by the Guards, should attack the left of the enemy near the sea. As General Hutchinson had a considerable circuit to make, the one attack was to be regulated by the other. When General Hutchinson reached the ground, he saw that the enemy's position was very strong, defended by a numerous artillery, and commanded by fortified hills near Alexandria. General Hutchinson halted, and sent to inform Sir Ralph that the heights could not be carried without considerable loss, and that if carried they would be exposed to the fire from the fortified hills, and could not be maintained without entrenchments, for which they had not the means. Beyond the hills on which the enemy were posted, nothing had hitherto been seen, and the information which had been received was doubtful and conflicting. Mr. Baldwin, the consul, stated that these hills were close to, and if possessed, would command the town of Alexandria. The Arabs, on the contrary, said that the hills were a considerable distance from Alexandria; that there was a plain of some extent between them, and a strong fortified position in front of the town. Sir Ralph went in person to examine the ground, and came to the conclusion that the Arabs were most probably correct in what they had stated, and however unwilling he might be to abandon the object which he had intended to effect, and to disappoint the hopes of the Army, who were flushed by their first success, prudence required that they should not persevere, and that the Army should be withdrawn and placed in a safe position. The event amply justified the wisdom of this decision, for the information of the Arabs proved to be perfectly correct. If the French had been driven back, they had Alexandria and a strong fortified position in front of it on which to retire, and which could not have been taken without heavy artillery and considerable delay. During the progress of this operation, the Army would have been exposed to a fire in front from Alexandria, and the fortified position, and to the danger of being attacked on the flank or rear by the troops which were expected from Cairo, and from the various detachments which had been called in.

The loss of officers and men in the engagement of the 13th of March was severe on both sides. The British had nearly 1100 rank and file killed or wounded.

So far the expedition had been successful. The landing, which the enemy confidently believed that they could resist, had been effected, water had been found, and Lake Maadieh, contrary to all the information that had been collected, was navigable for boats up to the canal of Alexandria. This last fact was the more important, as the weather had been so boisterous that there was scarcely a day on which stores could have been landed at Aboukir. The troops had displayed the strictest observance of discipline, the greatest quickness and precision in their movements, and the most undaunted bravery, for which they received the warm thanks of the commander in an order which he issued after the action of the 13th of March. The position occupied by the English Army was about four miles from Alexandria, and nine from Aboukir. The right was on the sea, and the left on the canal of Alexandria and the Lake, occupying a front of about a mile and a half. The ground on the right and centre was an irregular ridge of sand-hills, which gradually sloped into a plain in front of about a mile or three quarters in extent, which divided the two armies.

The Army was encamped in two lines, with the cavalry between them. The ground on which the reserve was posted was the most projecting part of the line, and between that corps and the brigade of Guards the ground fell into a hollow, through which the road from Alexandria to Aboukir passed. Behind the reserve were the remains of a large square building, of which the walls in many places were of considerable height, and in others afforded an excellent parapet.

The position of the enemy was also on a ridge of sand-hills, with the left to the sea, and the right towards a large tract of marshy ground, which, when overflowed by the Nile, is known as the Lake Mareotis.

As it was impossible to advance until the heavy artillery, and the requisites for conducting the siege of Alexandria had been brought up, orders were issued for strengthening the position of the Army. Two redoubts were begun on the canal of Alexandria, and a considerable *flèche* was thrown up in front of the reserve. The camp equipage was ordered to be landed, for hitherto there had not been a tent even for the commander. On the 17th of March, reports were received from several Arab chiefs that General Menou had left Cairo, with nearly the whole of the French force in Egypt, and had announced his intention of attacking the English as soon as he should reach Alexandria. It had been necessary to erect a breaching-battery against the castle of Aboukir, and after a resistance of two days, the defences were destroyed, and the garrison surrendered, and were immediately embarked for France. Early in the afternoon of the 18th of March, a strong patrol of the enemy's cavalry showed itself on the canal, and approached very near to the left. The cavalry pickets were ordered out, and were supported by a very considerable part of the brigade of cavalry. The officer in command, without reconnoitring what was in his front, gave the order to charge, and with horses so weak that they staggered under their riders, attacked the French dragoons, who, seeing that cavalry were their only assailants, prudently retired, posting a detachment behind a bank to arrest the progress of the English, who, both in advancing and retiring, suffered severely from its fire.

This check, though small to an army hitherto victorious, was very mortifying to Sir Ralph, who issued an order, strongly censuring the conduct of the cavalry, in which they were reminded, "that by thus undertaking enterprises without object and without use, they risked the lives of valuable men, and exposed themselves to failure."

On the 19th of March, the heavy ordnance, ammunition, and stores began to arrive, and the reports of General Menou's approach to Alexandria gained ground. The troops were ordered to be under arms every morning an hour before daybreak. On the 20th of March, Sir Ralph, in a conversation with General Moore, pointed out the difficulties which they had to encounter, and said, that as soon as the heavy guns were got up, and the entrenching tools were forwarded, it was his fixed purpose to make a great effort. His plan was to push forward the artillery in the night, and to form the troops under such cover as he could find, and at day-break to advance to the attack of both the enemy's flanks.

He said that in the event of failure, they could fall back on their present position, and maintain it until another could be prepared in the rear to favour their retreat, and, finally, their re-embarkation.

Although it had been reported that General Menou

was coming from Cairo with all the force he could collect, no authentic intelligence of his having reached Alexandria had been received. During the 20th of March nothing had been observed which indicated any stir or movement in the French camp. In the early part of the night a few rockets had been seen, but that was so common an occurrence, that it attracted no particular observation. General Moore, who had been the officer of the day on the 20th, remained with the picket of the reserve until four in the morning of the 21st March, and, as everything had been quiet during the night, he left orders with the field officer to retire his posts at daybreak. No immediate attack of the French was therefore expected on that morning, and no other precaution had been adopted than that enjoined by the general order issued on the 19th, by which the troops had been directed to be under arms every morning an hour before daylight. It was in consequence of this judicious arrangement that the troops had fortunately fallen in before the early attack of the French, on the morning of the 21st of March, commenced.[1]

[1] A copy of General Menou's orders was found in the pocket of General Loize, who was killed in the action of the 21st of March, from which it appeared that the plan of the French general was to make a false attack on the British left, while the real attack was to be directed against the right and centre, with the intention of driving the English into Lake Aboukir.

The action of the 21st of March began by a false attack on the part of the French on the British left, in which the enemy had a momentary and partial success, which was, however, promptly repaired, and they were repulsed with loss. The real attack, which was directed against the right and centre, speedily followed. The greatest efforts of the French were directed against the reserve, and it is therefore desirable to describe the exact position of that corps. The alarm posts of the 28th and 40th flank companies were in a redoubt which was open in the rear, and in which were placed two 24-pounders and several field-pieces. Two or three hundred yards behind the redoubt, but more to the right, and nearer to the sea, stood the old ruined building before mentioned, one side of which looked directly to the front, and commanded in a great degree the ground between the alarm posts of the 28th regiment and the sea. Here the 58th regiment was posted, and was covered against cannon shot. The 23d regiment occupied the front of the building on the left of the 58th, and looked to the rear of the 28th regiment, so as to keep in check any corps that might pass between the brigade of Guards and the left of the 28th regiment. The 42d regiment was encamped considerably in the rear, but had orders from General Moore to move up on the first alarm, and to form on the left of the 28th, placing its right to the ditch of the wall within which that regiment was placed.

The French drove in the pickets with great spirit and impetuosity, and a large column of infantry pressed forward close to the ditch of the redoubt, where, finding themselves vigorously opposed, they inclined to their right, passed round the left of the 28th regiment, and advanced towards that front of the old building where the 23d regiment was posted. The 42d regiment, which had not moved from its encampment until the firing had commenced, did not reach its post until the column of the French had penetrated thus far. By this means the enemy were placed between the 42d regiment and the old building. The 42d regiment was ordered to attack the enemy in the rear, and in the course of a very short time the French column was completely routed, and not a man escaped being killed, wounded, or taken prisoner.

The enemy made an attack on the centre, nearly at the same time with that which they had directed against the right of the English Army, but were repulsed with vigour and success. During the continuance of these struggles with the British right and centre, the fire of musketry and cannon was incessant and tremendous.

As the day began to dawn the enemy became sensible that they could not make any serious impression with their infantry, and they therefore decided to bring forward their cavalry. A column of at least 1000 cavalry advanced at full speed towards the left of the redoubt, where the 42d and General Stuart's regiment, which had been ordered from the second line to support the reserve, were drawn up in good order, and were at the time engaged with the infantry of the enemy. Although unable to check the velocity of this column of cavalry, the infantry were not dismayed but gave their fire, and allowed them to pass without quitting an inch of their ground. The 28th regiment faced its rear[1] rank to the right about, and threw in a destructive volley on the French cavalry, and the 23d regiment were so well posted behind the ruin of the old building, that without any risk they were enabled to check the progress of the enemy's squadrons, who, finding themselves attacked on all sides and without any hope of making a real impression, were glad to retreat, leaving a large number of their

---

[1] For this manœuvre the 28th regiment were authorized to bear the number of the regiment on the *back*, as well as on the front of their caps.

horses and men within the English line. Early in the action the regiments of Dillon and De Rolle had been ordered to occupy the vacant ground between the left of the reserve and the Guards in the centre, and by being so placed they were enabled to add greatly to the difficulties of the French cavalry in effecting their retreat. After this the enemy showed signs of being in much disorder, but they still kept up a heavy fire of musketry and artillery, and General Menou, unwilling to yield, resolved to make a last and desperate effort to repair the defeat he had sustained. For this purpose a considerable column of infantry was directed to attack the brigade of Guards, and at the same time the cavalry made a second charge on the reserve. The Guards reserved their fire until the enemy came close to their front, and then poured in such heavy discharges of musketry as speedily compelled them to retreat in the utmost disorder. The cavalry attacked nearly at the same place as on the former occasion, and they forced their way, as is not surprising, through the 42d and Stuart's regiments, which had been for a long time warmly engaged, and had lost a very great number both of officers and men. The troops in the ruin checked the progress of the cavalry, and the Minorca regiment, having been ordered out to support the 42d, General Roize made a desperate charge against it. This regiment allowed the French cavalry to pass, and then facing about poured such volleys upon them as brought many of the men and horses to the ground. The cavalry then endeavoured to force their way back, but were unable to do so. It is understood that General Roize had vainly attempted to dissuade General Menou from making this last effort, seeing that it could not possibly succeed, but his advice having been rejected, he executed his orders with the greatest spirit and courage, and fell in the struggle.

The enemy then began to collect their troops, and to draw them off by degrees, under the fire of their artillery.[1]

The object of General Menou had been to cut off the reserve which was a little advanced from the rest of the line; and if he had succeeded, the right of the English would have been turned, and their retreat in the face of a formidable cavalry, and of the commanding position he would have then occupied, would have been difficult and disastrous. But this object he was fortunately unable to effect, owing to the judicious disposition of the British troops, and of their undaunted bravery.

The safety of the English Army, the fate of Egypt, and the hopes of an honourable peace, were

[1] *Vide* Appendix D.

all involved in the result of this day's battle. These grave consequences must have been vividly present to the mind of the commander, who was devoting the last moments of his life with youthful ardour and zeal to the public service; whose thoughts were intently fixed on the security of an army, the discipline of which he had brought nearly to perfection, and who had long cherished an anxious desire for peace, as the greatest boon that could be conferred on his country, a glorious object, in the accomplishment of which, his own life was now about to be worthily closed.

The following remarks of General Moore furnish some details with regard to the personal conduct of Sir Ralph during this important battle:—" Sir Ralph had always been accused of exposing his person too much; I never knew him carry this so far as in this action. When it was so dark that I could scarcely distinguish, I saw him close to the rear of the 42d, without any of his family. He was afterwards joined by General Hope. When the French cavalry charged us for a second time, and our men were disordered, I called and waved with my hand to him to retire, but he was instantly surrounded by the hussars. He received a cut from a sabre on the breast which passed through his clothes, but only grazed the flesh. He must have been taken or killed, if a soldier had not shot the hussar."

It has never been ascertained at what precise time Sir Ralph received the wound which proved to be mortal. Colonel Abercromby states that his tent being at some distance from that of Sir Ralph, he did not see him when the first alarm of the French attack was given, and did not afterwards meet him until about break of day, in the rear of the reserve, when the principal attack had been made, and he then gave him orders relative to the movements of the troops. Colonel Abercromby did not afterwards see Sir Ralph until near the close of the action, when he found him in a small work about the centre of the line, where there were some guns firing on the enemy. Colonel Abercromby observed that the clothes of Sir Ralph were cut, and that there were marks of blood on them. He asked if he was wounded, and he answered, "Yes, by a spent ball, but it gives me no uneasiness," but he added that he felt considerable pain in his breast and side from a blow he had received from a French dragoon who rode against him, when the cavalry broke in on the right.

General Ludlow and Colonel Abercromby urged in the strongest manner that his wound should be examined, but he persevered in refusing, assigning as his reason, that there were many poor fellows worse wounded than he was, and that the surgeons were more usefully employed in attending to them. Sir Ralph dismounted, and walked about with apparent ease, watching earnestly the manœuvres of the enemy. After an interval of half an hour, he complained of being very faint, and sat down on the ground, with his back to the parapet of the redoubt.

General Ludlow then sent for one of the surgeons of the Guards, who were nearest at hand, but only a mate could be found. The mate looked at the wound, and found that the ball had entered the thigh, and Sir Ralph was again pressed to leave the field, but he would not do so until the firing had ceased, and the enemy had completely retired. As soon as the firing ceased, Sir Ralph was removed to the tent of Colonel Abercromby, where the wound was again examined by a skilful surgeon of the Guards, who, not finding the ball where he expected, advised that Sir Ralph should be carried on board a ship, to which he at once assented, and he was conveyed on board the "Foudroyant," Lord Keith's flag-ship. Sir Ralph was placed on a bier, and an officer who was present took a soldier's blanket, and was adjusting it under his head as a pillow, when Sir Ralph asked,

"What is that you are placing under my head?" The officer[1] replied that it was only a soldier's blanket, on which Sir Ralph said, "Only a soldier's blanket! a soldier's blanket is of great consequence, and you must send me the name of the soldier to whom it belongs, that it may be returned to him." This was accordingly done, and the blanket was duly restored, Sir Ralph himself having given directions to that effect.

Sir Ralph would not allow his son to accompany him to the beach, but frequently desired him to go to General Hutchinson, and to attend to his duty. Although the ball could not be extracted, sanguine hopes of recovery were entertained. On the 26th of March, the symptoms caused anxiety, but Sir Ralph rallied, and during the 27th he conversed with his son on various points connected with the public service with much composure, but in that night he became feverish, and at eleven o'clock on the night of the 28th of March he expired without pain or suffering.

The ball had taken a direction upwards, and had lodged in the thigh-bone, from whence it never could have been extracted. The body of Sir Ralph was sent to Malta, where it was interred, and a simple monument was erected over his grave.

[1] General Sir John Macdonald, late Adjutant-General of the Army.

It has been remarked, and no doubt with truth, by those who best knew Sir Ralph, that the circumstances attending his death were nearly such as he would have chosen for himself. The same sentiment has been thus beautifully expressed by one who did not personally know him : " Over Sir Ralph Abercromby I do not much lament; full of years and full of honour, he seems, with his own hands, to have erected a monument of glory, and then calmly entered it. When death must come, it never comes better than disguised as glory. Such ashes should rather be revered than deplored."

Sir Ralph, who always regarded unhesitating devotion to the public service as the first duty of a soldier, could not review his own career during the war, without a conscious feeling that neither unlooked for disappointment nor ultimate failure, which might have weighed with less elevated minds, had relaxed his untiring zeal and ardour in the cause of his country. He must have felt that he possessed in full measure the respect, the confidence, and the warmest attachment of the officers and soldiers under his command. He must have dwelt with unmingled satisfaction on the promptitude, precision, and good order with which all the movements of the troops had been conducted by the officers and men; the legitimate result of the just and rigid discipline which he had constantly enforced. Anticipated difficulties and serious deficiencies had been overcome, and the character of the British Army for discipline and valour had been raised and confirmed by three actions, which had been fought and won against a brave enemy, greatly superior in cavalry and artillery, and animated by the recollection of the splendid victories in which they had shared. Such are some of the reflections which must have soothed and cheered the dying moments of the veteran commander.

Sir Ralph died too soon to know the full extent of the service he had rendered to his country. He did not live to know that the battle of the 21st March virtually decided the fate of Egypt, and facilitated the conclusion of peace, for which he so ardently wished. The importance of this service is now understood, and is appreciated by the rapid communication through Egypt which is maintained between England and her possessions in the East; and, if the day should ever arrive, as arrive it may, when Egypt shall again become the battle-field, there is no reason to doubt that the interest and honour of the country will be maintained with equal skill and valour, and crowned with equal success.

CHAPTER VIII.

CONCLUSION.

THE preceding narrative has been conducted with an anxious desire to adhere to unexaggerated simplicity, and with a scrupulous respect for truth, in the belief that the facts disclosed would afford the surest means of estimating the private virtues and the public services of Sir Ralph. I dare not venture to give expression to my own view of his character; I cannot be a competent judge of his military skill and science, and my unabated remembrance of his kindness and affection as a parent, disqualify me from being an impartial judge of the other qualities which marked his pure, sagacious, and elevated character. I must therefore, as I have before done, appeal to the authority and opinions of others, and to a reference to some of the prominent acts of his life.

A distinguished general officer, who, from his laborious study of the art of war as a science, was more capable than most men of his time to appreciate the merits of a commander, who thoroughly knew Sir Ralph, was intimately acquainted with his opinions, and had the closest opportunity of seeing his conduct on service, has ascribed to him " the most perfect knowledge of his profession in all its branches, from the highest parts of the art of war to the details of a garrison, or camp, or regimental duty, which he had acquired by careful and diligent study of the duties of a soldier; a perfectly clear and combining head, great firmness of purpose, and extraordinary sagacity in happily conjecturing the designs of an adversary from slight indications." His valour, of course, he placed among the inferior qualities of the captain, and he added that, while Sir Ralph felt this, and always in conversation maintained that the commander's duty was to keep himself out of fire, he owned that he never could prevail upon himself to obey his own rule. When the fight began he seemed to be uneasy and impatient until he reached the point where the struggle raged most fiercely, and then he was at ease, and he became more collected, clear, and decisive in giving his orders as the perils around him increased. Sir Ralph was very short-sighted, and this he considered to be the only deficiency in his military capacity, and to this he attributed, in part, his so constantly exposing his own person. It was the unhesitating opinion of this general officer that, if Sir Ralph had been supported and placed in circumstances at all similar to those of other most distinguished commanders, he must have acquired the greatest military renown. He enlarged on the extraordinary skill and foresight which were displayed in the arrangements for landing in Egypt, which was a combined naval and military operation, a service of unusual difficulty, calling forth all the talents and resolution of a general. He had the highest opinion of Sir Ralph's political wisdom, founded on an intimate knowledge of his opinions, and he fondly dwelt on the perfect and exemplary independence of his conduct towards the Government which he served, as illustrated by various instances, which proved how plainly, at all periods of his life, he spoke truth, however unpleasant to those who employed him. He regarded the private worth of Sir Ralph as something so pure, that it almost defied panegyric.[1]

It will remain for those who have followed the course of Sir Ralph, to judge how far this view

[1] For these recollections of Sir Ralph I am indebted to the kindness of a friend, who embodied them as the substance of repeated conversations with the general officer whose opinion and judgment they express.

of his conduct, capacity, and character, has been justified and confirmed by his acts, and by the whole tenor of his life.

His military merits secured for him in the highest measure the respect and attachment of the Army, and the entire confidence of his Government. His political wisdom was proved by his early appreciation of the true nature of the principles of that conflict which was convulsing Europe; and his love of order and respect for the law, combined with kindness and justice to the people, were evinced by his conduct in Ireland. His indignant rejection of pecuniary rewards, which he deemed to be undignified, and his refusal of high rank, because it had not been earned in a service which had ended in the advantage and glory of his country, prove the purity of his character, and show that his love of distinction and of fame was regulated by the noblest standard. His exercise of power was considerate and just, and untainted by caprice, temper, or partiality; and he performed all the duties of domestic life with the same constancy, kindness, and simplicity which characterized his public career. The singular modesty of his nature restrained him from making any allusion to his own services, even in the most select circles, and the proud reliance with which he reposed on the consciousness of the zeal, disinterestedness, and purity which governed his actions, have led to his character being hitherto less understood, and his merits less appreciated than they deserved to be.

An attempt has now been made to supply, however inadequately, this defect, and if it is in any degree successful in illustrating and developing the real character of Sir Ralph, it will be the best justification of an effort which has been prompted by the warmest and deepest feelings of affection, gratitude, and veneration.

The notice of the life of Sir Ralph Abercromby cannot be more aptly concluded than by these words from the general order issued by the Duke of York, on the occasion of the victory of the 21st March 1801 :—

"The illustrious example of their commander cannot fail to have made an indelible impression on the gallant troops at whose head, crowned with victory and glory, he terminated his honourable career; and his Majesty trusts that a due contemplation of the talents and virtues which he uniformly displayed in the course of his valuable life, will for ever endear the memory of Sir Ralph Abercromby to the British Army. . . .

"His steady observance of discipline, his ever-watchful attention to the health and wants of his troops, the persevering and unconquerable spirit which marked his military career, the splendour of his actions in the field, and the heroism of his death, are worthy the imitation of all who desire, like him, a life of honour and a death of glory."

APPENDIX.

APPENDIX.

Appendix A.—P. 252.

Memorial communicated by Lieutenant-General Sir Ralph Abercromby to the English Government, on the Liberation of the Spanish Provinces in South America.

The people of Great Britain in general take little concern in the affairs of foreign nations. The balance of Europe is a subject they do not understand; and they are little interested in anything that does not tend to the security and extension of commerce, and to the dominion of the sea.

To keep up the spirits of the nation, and to engage it heartily in the further prosecution of the war, it seems necessary that every military enterprise we shall undertake, shall be directed to such objects as shall tend to secure to us, or to enlarge, the sources of our commerce and wealth.

With this view, it has occurred that the removal of the French from Egypt should be effected before a negotiation for peace should take place. To allow it to remain in their possession would threaten the security of our dominions in the East; at any rate, were the cession of it to become an object of discussion at the peace, a considerable degree of weight would be given to it in the general scale, and concessions would be demanded of more consequence than we would be inclined to grant.

But of all the objects which ought to claim our attention, the liberation of South America from the dominion of Spain seems to stand first. It can only be effected whilst we are still at war with Spain, and if it should be happily accomplished, it would be beyond the reach of negotiation at a peace.

It should be undertaken without any view to conquest, to exclusive commerce, or to plunder. Every port in South America, and the whole trade of that extensive continent should be declared free; every country would feel interested in it (Spain and Portugal excepted).

Great Britain, however, from her enterprise, from her capital, and from her industry, would in reality possess nine parts in ten of this great commerce. A market would be equally opened for British and for East India commodities. In a short time the Brazils (which would follow the fate of the Spanish settlements in South America), and the other countries now under the dominion of Spain, would produce more sugar, cotton, and indigo, than all of our West India islands, and at a cheaper rate. By degrees we should be enabled to drop our sugar islands, which we retain at a great expense, and which are frequently the source of wars.

Should Great Britain decline at this time to undertake this great enterprise, some other nation will attempt it on principles less liberal, and less advantageous to the happiness of South America, and to the world at large.

The present state of that country gives us reason to believe that it would not be difficult to accomplish this object.

APPENDIX. 313

The Creole Spaniards and Indians are oppressed beyond measure. No office can be held in that part of the world but by a native of old Spain, and the restrictions on trade are severe in the extreme. Justice is venal, and extortion commonly practised by all in power. The clergy, who have great influence over an ignorant and superstitious people, are in general natives of New Spain, and consequently would favour a revolution. It seems only necessary that we should remove the Spanish forces; declare to the people what our intentions are, and the Spanish government would fall to the ground.

Two expeditions should be fitted out,—one to proceed to the Cape of Good Hope, and from thence to the river Plate; the other should rendezvous at Barbadoes, on the Gulf of Paria, and should act on the provinces of Cumana, the Caraccas, and Venezuela.

Monte Video is the principal port and rendezvous for shipping in the river Plate. It is situated on the left bank of that great river; Buenos Ayres, the capital of the country, is situated on the right. One or two line-of-battle ships, and as many frigates, are commonly stationed at Monte Video, and two battalions of Spanish infantry at Buenos Ayres, for the defence of that country. Of the force at Monte Video little is known.

The approach to Buenos Ayres by water, can only be made in vessels of a small draught, on account of the shoals. The climate is good, and the country abounds in provisions. Roads have been opened across the country to Chili and Peru, and European commodities are carried over land into those provinces, which are paid for in specie, and brought from Buenos Ayres to Europe.

The expedition against the Terra Firma should act in

the rivers Orinoco and Guarapichi, and against La Guayra, and Porto Cabello; the above-mentioned rivers give an opening into the province of Cumana.

La Guayra is the port of St. Juan de Leon of the Caraccas, it covers the approach to that great capital, and is strongly fortified to the sea. A landing, however, may be effected to the right or left of La Guayra, particularly at the small river Tuy, and if the batteries to the sea can be turned (which they probably may) this fortress would soon fall, and consequently the capital of the province.

Porto Cabello is said to be a place of considerable strength, but probably like La Guayra it is not equally strong on the land side as on the water.

It may admit of a doubt whether in carrying on these operations, we should do more than blockade those fortresses, taking it for granted, that as soon as the revolution had taken effect they would surrender; but it is to be apprehended, that a people who possess so little energy as the Creole Spaniards would not venture to adopt so decided a measure as throwing off the Spanish yoke until they saw their enemies removed, and British garrisons in La Guayra and Porto Cabello.

If a revolution could be set fairly on foot in the principal settlements on the coast, it would spread with rapidity into the interior of the country. Emissaries would be sent to propagate the joyful event, and to assure them that the British troops should not quit the country till relieved from the Spanish yoke, and until a new Government of their own should be established. All that would be required on the part of Great Britain in the first instance would be, to furnish them with arms and ammunition, and to assist them in framing a form of Government best suited to the genius and temper of the people.

Much information and many details will be necessary before these undertakings can be set on foot. Captain M'Dowall of the Ganges (who was an Admiral in the Portuguese service when Portugal endeavoured to establish a colony at St. Sacrement) certainly knows the navigation of the river Plate ; and amongst the Spanish prisoners now in England, with a little address, some of them may be found who can give pretty accurate knowledge of the river Plate and of the coasts of Terra Firma, and General Miranda is still in London.

Lieutenant-Colonel Picton, the Commandant of Trinidad, was instructed, in 1797, to procure every possible information relative to the neighbouring provinces of Cumana, the Caraccas, and Venezuela, and Colonel Maitland might be directed to go to Trinidad to arrange with Colonel Picton the plan of operations.

The province of Guyana is already nearly in our possession ; there remains, however, in the possession of the French the small island of Cayenne, and some inconsiderable plantations on the mainland ; it may be necessary to root out the French by removing the garrison, and the French settlers in this island, and by a total destruction of the fort, and adjacent town.

To insure the success of this great enterprise a very considerable force (probably not less than 12,000 men) would be required. Were it to fail, the unfortunate natives would be left to the merciless revenge of their cruel masters, and many of them would end their days on the scaffold, or in the mines.

The difficulty seems to be to find a sufficient disposable force; this, however, may be procured, provided the general principles in which this enterprise is founded shall be approved of.

Nothing has been said of Mexico. Unless the Americans were to co-operate we have not a sufficient force to favour a revolution in that part of the Spanish settlements; the probability however is, that the same spirit would prevail through that great continent.

APPENDIX B.—P. 257.

DESPATCH FROM LIEUTENANT-GENERAL SIR RALPH ABERCROMBY TO RIGHT HONOURABLE MR. DUNDAS.

LA VALETTE, MALTA, *December* 9, 1800.

SIR,—Were I to enter fully into a statement of the military and civil establishment of Malta, and so detail circumstantially the prodigious works with which the town and harbour of La Valette are surrounded, I should exceed the bounds of a letter. I have directed the engineers to make out a report on the fortifications, which, as soon as completed, shall be transmitted to England with an accompanying plan. Captain Ball, of the Navy, who has acted here as Civil Governor, has desired that I would permit him to transmit such papers as will explain the nature of the Civil Government and the Revenue of the Island.

As a military station, it may be pronounced to be the most complete in His Majesty's possession, and the harbour, which is capacious and perfectly safe, is perhaps the best port in the Mediterranean; the works are so contrived as to cover the harbour, so that it scarcely can be subject to any attack, and must remain a safe arsenal and a complete dockyard for the Navy, until the place itself shall be forced to surrender, which can only be effected after a long and laborious siege.

Although the works are in themselves very extensive, yet it does not appear that a very numerous garrison is required, and were any of the outworks to be abandoned, or to fall into the hand of the enemy, yet the body of the place might be long defended. An invading enemy can only approach the island on two points, in the Bay of St. Paul's and its neighbourhood, and in the Bay of Marsa, Sirocco. Whilst the existing batteries are kept in repair, it will be next to impossible for any ship to come to an anchor in either of those bays, but the great strength of the island must be considered to consist in the attachment of the inhabitants, and the difficulty of the country, every field of two or three acres being enclosed with high stone walls.

The inhabitants are a brave, active, hardy race, and if they can once be firmly attached to the Government under which they live, it will be extremely difficult to wrest Malta out of its possession. I am sorry to say, that hitherto they appear to have been very ill governed. The Knights were bad masters. Justice was perverted whenever they found it convenient. The income of the Judges arose principally from fees, and the Grand-Master had made a monopoly of corn, and of all the mills of the country. No person was permitted to import a sack of grain except a corporation consisting of four persons named by the Grand-Master and acting under him. All the corn was lodged in the town of La Valette, and every individual was obliged to purchase it there, and to grind it at the Grand-Master's mills.

The corn was retailed at one-third more than it cost, except in years of scarcity, when it was sold at the usual price, but as this happens seldom, from the vicinity to the fruitful island of Sicily, the Grand-Master drew a revenue to himself of between twenty and thirty thousand pounds a year, one year with another, independent of the regular revenue of the island, amounting to about thirty-six thousand pounds per annum, arising from landed property in the island belonging to the order; from the rent of windmills, houses, and warehouses in town; from customs and a tax on wine; from a tax of three and a half per cent. on the sale of property, and from the Mont-de-Piété, or pawnbroker's shop. All this is at present under the administration of Captain Ball, who is an exceedingly honourable man; but as he is in the hands of a few people in the island, who certainly may take an advantage if they please, it appears necessary that some steps should be taken to establish a British system of administration, without altering, perhaps, for the present the usual forms of administering justice, or of receiving the revenue.

If the island should remain with Great Britain, such alteration may take place as may relieve the inhabitants from an oppressive monopoly, and from the perversion of justice. Hitherto no merchant has been ever able to establish himself in Malta, and whoever shall be appointed Governor of the island for the time being, must continue to import grain for the sustenance of the inhabitants till such time as a free importation can be established; and at all times it will be necessary to have a stock of provisions for the garrison for at least eight months.

I should apprehend that if an intelligent and honest British commissary and English secretary for the island were sent out, the Governor, whoever he may be, with the assistance of some person or persons of respectability in the island, would be able to carry on the affairs of the government, leaving the courts of justice in their present form, keeping a strict eye over them, and as all decisions and appeals must naturally come before him, he will soon perceive how justice is administered. It certainly might be right to give the judges fixed salaries out of the revenues of the island, and to take away all perquisites.

It is necessary to explain the situation in which Captain Ball at present stands. On the revolt of the island, in September 1798, he was sent by Lord Nelson and the Court of Naples to attend to the interest of his Sicilian Majesty; and until the surrender of the town of La Valette, every public act was in the name of the King of the Two Sicilies, the Sicilian colours were everywhere hoisted, and at this moment they are flying in most parts of the island. If Captain Ball has received any salary, it has been from his Sicilian Majesty. His table has been kept at the expense of the island. Having, in obedience to Lord Nelson's orders, given up his professional pursuits, he has reaped no benefit from prize-money, and has only received bare pay as Captain of the "Alexander;" his situation seems now incompatible with that of Major-General Pigot's, and I hope that some decision will take place. I feel great delicacy in removing Captain Ball; at the same time, I am obliged to place all authority in the hands of Major-General Pigot, and to direct him to employ Captain Ball in the administration of the civil affairs of the island until his Majesty's pleasure is known.

I trust that the honourable conduct of Captain Ball (who from every account has given general satisfaction to the inhabitants) will recommend him for some consideration for his services, and that any irregularity which may have taken place in his acting in the name of his Sicilian Majesty, may not be imputed to him.

It may be expected from my situation that I should say a few words on the importance of this island to Great Britain, and of the relative advantages of Malta and Minorca in a military point of view. During the summer, I seriously considered the situation of Minorca, and the only conclusion that I could draw was, that, although the harbour must be acknowledged to be excellent, and its situation convenient to control the naval power of France and Spain, and so prevent them from passing the Straits of Gibraltar without our knowledge, yet it appeared to me that no skill of the ablest engineer could protect it and the dockyard, and that in the commencement of a war, it is always in the power of France and Spain to invade that island, and either to take it from us or to destroy the dockyard; to this may be added, that the fortifications of Fort St. Philip's are a heap of ruins, that the present temporary works can only serve as retreat for the troops to entitle them to a capitulation, and that if we shall keep the island, all the fortifications must be reconstructed.

Malta, in point of situation, does not possess the advantages of Minorca, and is not so convenient a station for a fleet in time of war, yet possessing so many other advantages, it may almost, on a comparison, be equal, if not superior; and if it were to fall into the hands of a powerful enemy, we should severely feel the consequences of it. To France, it would afford an opportunity of again attempting an establishment in Egypt; and to Russia, it would become a depôt of naval stores for the powers in the Mediterranean who are hostile to us, and might give to either of these powers a preponderance in the Mediterranean, and the means of weakening the Turkish empire. Whether Malta, in a commercial light, would be considered of consequence to Great Britain, is very uncertain. The inhabitants carry on a manufacture in cotton to a considerable extent, which interferes with ours. It is not probable that it would become a great depôt for British goods. British commodities would be carried directly to Genoa, Leghorn, Naples, Messina, Smyrna, and Constantinople. It is possible, indeed, that the Barbary States might take from Malta such goods as they might want, and that a few Jews from Tunis and Tripoli, and a few Greeks from the Archipelago, might establish themselves at Malta, and carry on a small commerce.

The revenue of Malta, it must be allowed, would go a considerable way to defray the expense of the establishment, and in course of time, we might draw from it recruits for our Army and Navy, as the island is very populous, and probably would become more so under our Government.

I beg pardon for taking up so much of your time in a long letter, which might have been more distinct and concise if I had not been otherwise much employed.—I have the honour to be, etc., R. A.

THE RIGHT HONOURABLE HENRY DUNDAS, ETC.

APPENDIX C.—P. 259.

THE Bay of Marmorice, on the coast of Caramania, was judiciously selected as the third rendezvous for the Fleet.

The entrance to the Bay is not many hundred yards in breadth, but within, its circumference is twenty miles. The depth of water is everywhere sufficient for ships of the largest size, and it is surrounded by high mountains covered to the summit with the finest wood; and many small rivers discharge themselves into the Bay. The safety of the Fleet was secured. There was abundance of wood and water, and within a few days' sail of Egypt.

Appendix D.—P. 296.

THE enemy had assembled the whole of his force with the exception of one demi-brigade and one regiment of cavalry, expecting, perhaps not unreasonably, that by a great effort he might put an end to the contest. According to the best accounts, the enemy brought into the field at least 12,000 infantry and 1500 cavalry. Their artillery was numerous and well served. The force of the English army did not exceed 10,000 infantry and 300 cavalry. The artillery was not numerous, and from defective means of transport the guns were for some time without ammunition. The loss of the English was 1464 killed, wounded, and missing. Generals Hope, Moore, Oakes, and Colonel Paget were wounded. The French lost at least 3000 men, probably more. Generals Lanusse, Roize, and Baudot were killed; Generals Destaing, Silly, Eppler, and others were wounded.

INDEX.

INDEX.

ABERCROMBY, family, sketch of, 13-15.
Abercromby, General Sir Robert, 25.
Abercromby, Lieut.-General Sir John, use made of his journal, 10, 273; remarks on the attempted landing at Cadiz, 232.
Aboukir, advantages of, for disembarkation, 263.
Alloa school, 15, 17.
America, South, independence of, a favourite project, 57, 252, 311-316.
American Independence, War of, 5, 19-23.
Amiens, Peace of, 3.
Anstruther, Colonel, 260.
Arabs, friendly services of the, to the English camp in Egypt, 282, 286.
Army, inefficiency and disorganization of, in early part of the war, 4, 7; efforts for its regeneration successful, 8, 9.
Austrians, the, in Flanders, 48, 49.

BALDWIN, Mr., British consul at Cairo and Alexandria, 264, 282, 286.
Bar, Scotch, father and grandfather members of, 15.
Battle of the "Diamond," 62.
Berbice, surrender of, 55.
Bergen, attack on, 187.
Bois de Bohain, attack on the, 47.
Borstel, General, 193.
Brownrigg, Colonel, 145.
Brune, General, 169, 189.

CADIZ, expedition against, 219-239; embarkation at Portsmouth, 221; subsequent movements, 222-226;
sailing of the Fleet from Minorca under Lord Keith, 226; difficulties in carrying out their instructions, 227-230; ineffective arrangements made for landing, 230, 231; abandonment of the enterprise, 233-237.
Calvert, Sir Henry, 42, 43, 45.
Camden, Lord, Lord-Lieutenant in Ireland, 31; state of the country under his administration, 61, 71. *See* Ireland.
Capture of a French corvette in the Mediterranean, 269.
Carhampton, Lord, 63, 71.
Castlereagh, Lord, 61, 136.
Cavan, Lord, 284.
Christian, Admiral, 54.
Clackmannan, became M.P. for county of, 23.
Classics (Latin), familiarity with, 29.
Cochrane, Captain, 277, 280.
College, student at, 16.
Colonelcy in King's Irish Infantry, or 103d Regiment, 19.
Commander, Sir Ralph's skill as a, 303-306.
Conway, General, 21.
Coote, General, 279.
Cornetcy, purchase of, in Third Dragoon Guards, 18.
Cornwallis, Lord, 124.
Correspondence with Ministers of Crown, 5.
Council of war, in campaign in Holland, 184.
Cradock, Major-General, 284.
Cuyler, General, 60.

DAENDALS, General, 169, 178.
Daer, Basil Lord, 36, 37.

INDEX.

Death of Sir Ralph, 300.
Declaration of war against England and Holland by France, 39.
Demerara, surrender of, 55.
Discipline, Army, 7-9, 43, 44.
Don, General, 176.
Duff, Mr., of Braco, 13.
Duke of York, 4; *see* York.
Duncan, Lord, 156, 168.
Dundas, Mr., Secretary-at-War, correspondence with, on the campaign in Flanders, 46; on command in West Indies, 59; on the command in Ireland, 106, 107, 114; as to the expedition to Holland, 144, 148-157, 162, 173, 174, 180, *et seq.*; on the expedition to Cadiz, 219; his views regarding the possession of Egypt, 243-249, 251, *et seq.*
Dundas, Mr., of Manor, maternal grandfather, 15.
Dundas, Professor, 14.
Dundas, Sir David, 184, 191, 198.
Dundas, Sir Laurence, 24.
Dunkirk, defeat of the attack on, 45.
Dutch Fleet, surrender of the, 172.

EDINBURGH, life at, 29, 30.
Education and early life, 15, 17.
Effingham, Lord, 21.
Egmont, battle at, 190-194.
Egypt, expedition to, 240-302; motives to this enterprise, 243-249; effective strength of the Army for this service, 254; sailing of the Fleet from Gibraltar, 256; Malta and Marmorice Bay, 256-260; state of the Turkish army, 260-263; paucity of information as to Egypt, 257, 263-267; Sir Ralph's views of the prospects of the expedition, 267, 268; departure of the Fleet from Marmorice Bay, 273; arrival in Aboukir Bay, 275; difficulties experienced in landing, 275-278; details of the subsequent struggle, 278-291; force of the respective armies, 322; narrative of the decisive action on 21st March, 292-296; Sir Ralph's conduct during this battle, 297, 298; his fatal wound, and death on the 28th, 298-300.
Elgin, Lord, 17.
Elgin, Lord, ambassador at Constantinople, 267.

Embarkation for Holland, 42.
Erskine, Colonel, contest with, as to Clackmannanshire election, 23, 24.
Erskine, Sir William, 47.
Essen, General, 191, 193.
European War, views regarding it, 46, 160, 161.
Evacuation of Holland, 52.
Expedition to the West Indies, 54-60.

FAME, views of, 5, 6.
Family and early life, 13-38.
Ferdinand, Prince, of Brunswick, service under, 4, 40.
First night of Sir Ralph in Egypt, 281.
Fitzwilliam, Lord, 61.
Flanders, campaign in, 39-53; appointed to command a brigade, 41; miserable inefficiency of the men described, 42, 43; advance of the Allies, 47-50; close of the campaign, 50-53.
Fletcher, Captain, 274.
Fox, General, 49, 223.
Frederick of Prussia, 33, 40.
French Fleet sent to Ireland, 64; dispersion of, 65.
French Revolution, views of, 30-34, 46.
Friant, General, 275.
Furnes, attack on the camp of, 44.

GERMANY, went to, with Third Dragoon Guards, 18, 19.
"Glory," the, voyage of, 55.
Gosford, Lord, 62.
Grattan, Mr., 67.

HALL, Lieutenant-Colonel, 281.
Hardy, Professor, 30.
Helder, attack on the, 171.
Hermann, General, 184, 187; captured in the attack on Bergen, 187, 189.
Holland, expedition to, 139-218; views of its projectors, 139, 140; hazards of the enterprise, 141-143; proposals of Ministers, 145-147; views of Sir Ralph, 147-149, 161-164; conflicting instructions as to the campaign, 149-157; impracticability of the plans of attack proposed, 157-160; sailing of the expedition, 163, 168; attack on the Helder, and cap-

INDEX.

ture of the Dutch Fleet, 169-172; subsequent difficulties, 175; arrival of reinforcements, 176; apathy of the Dutch, 178, 185, 190; engagement at Potten, 179; command surrendered to the Duke of York, 180, 184; arrival of the Russian forces, 184; attack on Bergen, 187; loss in this action, 189; battle at Egmont, 190-194; review of the expedition at this stage, 194; last action in this enterprise, 195; abandonment of the expedition, 196; re-occupation of the Zype, 197; correspondence on closing the campaign, and returning to Britain, 198-208; Sir Ralph rejoins his family in Scotland, 210.
Hopetoun, Lord, 8.
Howe, Lord, 21.
Hutchinson, Lord, letter from, 135-138.

IRELAND, serves there with Third Dragoon Guards, 19; state of the country under Lord Camden's administration, 61-71; disorganization of the Army, 71; Sir Ralph succeeds Lord Carhampton in the command, 71; difficulties with which he had to contend, 72-75; instructions issued to officers, 76-80; his policy distasteful to Camden and his advisers, 75, 76, 80, 85, 88, 89, 110, 121; letters to Mr. Elliot and the Duke of York on the subject, 82-85; visit to the south, and the result of his observations, 85-87, 92; the celebrated order of 26th February 1798, 93, 94; Camden's vacillating policy, 94-96; inspection of the Army in the north, 97; alarm and opposition consequent on this, 98-106; Sir Ralph's resolution to resign, 106, 107; correspondence on the subject, 107-115; General Lake's appointment to the command, 122; Sir Ralph's conduct throughout approved by the King and his Ministers, 123-125.
Irish Parliament of 1797, 66-68.

JOMINI, General, quoted on state of the Army, 7, 8, 43.

KAIMITZ, General, 48.
Keith, Lord, 229; difficulties between him and Sir Ralph as to landing at Cadiz, 229-237.
Kempt, General Sir James, 162, 182.
Kennet, Lord, Judge of Court of Session, 23.
Keppel, Admiral, 21.
King, anecdote of the, 125.

LANDING of the troops at Aboukir, 276, 277.
Law, dislike to the study of, 17.
Leipsic, study of civil law at, 17.
London, freedom of the city bestowed on Sir Ralph, 183.

MACDONALD, General Sir John, 300.
M'Kerras, Major, 274.
M'Nevin, Dr., 61, 66, 68.
Mar, Earl of, 23.
Malta, blockade of, 222; surrender, 224. See Minorca.
Marengo, battle of, 223.
Marmorice Bay, 259, 321.
Marriage, 26.
Martinet, General, 279.
Mediterranean, command in the, accepted, 221.
Melas, General, 222.
Menou, General, advance of, 289, 295, 296.
Menzies, Mr., of Ferton, 26.
Military life, active, summarized, 4; entrance on, 18; sketch of, down to 1783, 19.
Minorca and Malta, their comparative value to England, 257, 316-321.
Mitchell, Admiral, 168, 181.
Moir, Mr., teacher at Alloa, 15.
Moira, Lord, 97, 98.
Moore, General, 171; his account of the attempted landing at Cadiz, 231; his views on the expedition to Egypt, 241, 242.
Murray, Lieut.-Col., 260.

NAPLES, application by the Queen to Sir Ralph to undertake its defence, 224.

OAKES, General, 278.

INDEX.

"Only a soldier's blanket!" 300.
Otto, General, 49.

PARLIAMENTARY life, views of, 25.
Parliament, debates in, as to the expedition to Holland, 211.
Peerage offered to Sir Ralph, but declined, 212-216.
Pelham, Mr., 111-113, 121.
Picton, Sir Thomas, 57.
Pitt, General Sir William, 19, 40.
Pitt, Mr., 212, 214, 217.
Political differences, 36, 37.
Popular favour, not courted, 6.
Portland, Duke of, 100, 105, 113, 132.
Porto Rico, attack on, 56, 58.
Portugal, threatened invasion of, by Spain, 220.
Potten, importance of the position, 177.
Private habits and pursuits, 26-30.
Prussia, policy of, in regard to the expedition to Holland, 145-147, 166.
Pulteney, General Sir James, 170, 174, 183, 226.

RICHARDSON, Lieutenant, 280.
Rugby, pupil at, 16.
Roize, General, 291, 295, 296.
Russia, treaty of, with England, 139. 166; arrival of the Russian forces in Holland, 184; repulse of the attack on Bergen, 187.

SCOTLAND, appointment as Commander of the Forces in, 134.
Smith, Sir Sidney, 275.
St. Lucie, attack on, 55.
St. Vincent's, 55.
Stuart, General Sir Charles, 219.
Summary of military service, 4.
Syme, Rev. Mr., 15.

TITLE, proposal to bestow, on Sir Ralph, 212; his refusal, 213.
Tone, Mr. Wolfe, 64.
Treaty between Russia and England, 139; its object, 208.
Trinidad, successful attack on, 56.
Tullibody, estate of, 13, 14; village, 28.
Turkish army incapable of co-operating with the English in Egypt, 260.

UNIVERSITY of Edinburgh, attendance at, 16.

VALENCIENNES, storming of, 44.
Vandamme, General, 193.
Vaux, the Allies' attack on, 47.

WAR with America and that with France contrasted, 19-23.
Washington, General, 20, 31.
West Indies, command in the, 4, 54-60; difficulties and disasters attending the first campaign, 55; success of the second expedition, with a view to attack the Spanish possessions, 56, 57; failure at Porto Rico, 58-60.

YORK, Duke of, 4; his command of the campaign in Flanders, 41; opposed to besieging Dunkirk, 45; letter to, on resigning the command in Ireland, 111; command of the expedition to Holland, 139, 145, 180, 183; his encomium on Sir Ralph, 307, 308.
Yorke, Sir Joseph, 17.

ZUYDER ZEE, 176.

www.ingramcontent.com/pod-product-compliance
Lightning Source LLC
Chambersburg PA
CBHW031133160426
43193CB00008B/124